Frank Hatchett's
Jazz Dance

Frank Hatchett's Jazz Dance

Frank Hatchett

Broadway Dance Center
New York City, NY

Nancy Myers Gitlin

Lake Michigan College
Benton Harbor, MI

Human Kinetics

Library of Congress Cataloging-in-Publication Data

Hatchett, Frank.
    Frank Hatchett's jazz dance / Frank Hatchett, Nancy Myers Gitlin.
        p. cm.
    Includes bibliographical references.
    ISBN 0-7360-0025-9
    1. Jazz dance. I. Title: Jazz dance. II. Gitlin, Nancy Myers, 1962- III. Title.

GV1753 . H38 2000
793.3--dc21

99-046848

ISBN: 0-7360-0025-9

Acquisitions Editor: Judy Patterson Wright, PhD
Managing Editor: Cynthia McEntire
Assistant Editor: John Wentworth
Copyeditor: Amie Bell
Proofreader: Joanna Hatzopoulos
Graphic Designer: Robert Reuther
Graphic Artist: Francine Hamerski
Photo Editor: Clark Brooks
Cover Designer: Keith Blomberg
Cover Photographer: (background) Cover Photo: Eduardo Patino, NYC; (foreground) Photo by Harvey Kushner courtesy of Dance Olympus.
Photographers (interior): All photos by Rick Stone except: page vi © Ron P. Jaffe/Unicorn Stock Photos; pages ix, 10, and 158 photos by Dori Sullivan; pages 5 and 12 photos by Warren Myers; page 6 © Viren Desai/Unicorn Stock Photos; pages vii and 1 photos courtesy of Broadway Dance Center, New York. Author photo of Frank Hatchett by Roy Blakey. Author photo of Nancy Myers Gitlin by Rick Stone.
Medical Illustrator: Elizabeth Young
Models: Nancy Myers Gitlin and Jason Warley
Printer: Versa Press

Human Kinetics

Web site: http://www.humankinetics.com/

United States: Human Kinetics
P.O. Box 5076
Champaign, IL 61825-5076
1-800-747-4457
e-mail: humank@hkusa.com

Canada: Human Kinetics
475 Devonshire Road Unit 100
Windsor, ON N8Y 2L5
1-800-465-7301 (in Canada only)
e-mail: humank@hkcanada.com

Europe: Human Kinetics, P.O. Box IW14
Leeds LS16 6TR, United Kingdom
+44 (0)113-278 1708
e-mail: humank@hkeurope.com

Australia: Human Kinetics
57A Price Avenue
Lower Mitcham, South Australia 5062
(08) 82771555
e-mail: liah@senet.com.au

New Zealand: Human Kinetics
P.O. Box 105-231, Auckland Central
09-523-3462
e-mail: humank@hknewz.com

For my grandmother, Mrs. Mamie Brandon, and my parents, Mr. and Mrs. Frank Hatchett.

—Frank Hatchett

For my husband, Josh, truly the wind beneath my wings; my sons Alex and Matthew, who had a world of patience and even more love; and my parents, Marlene and Warren, my guiding lights.

—Nancy Myers Gitlin

Contents

VOP is a spirit, a flavoring, a passion, and an attitude. Learn how Frank fused influences from other dance forms and the rhythm of life to create the Hatchett style.

Projection communicates, focus directs, attitude counts, energy motivates, music matters, flavor enhances, and fusion connects to create the spirit of the dance.

Foreword

Frank Hatchett with Brooke Shields and Grace Wakefield.

Flavor: n. *1. distinctive taste; 2. the characteristic quality of a thing.*

I came to the Broadway Dance Center for the first time at age 19, the summer after my freshman year in college. I always loved dancing but had never pursued it professionally. During university, however, I was accepted to a theater company that used quite a bit of dancing in its programs. The actors were divided into two groups: the "dancer-dancers" and the background dancers. My dancing ability at the time solidified my position as a background dancer. I watched and envied the dancer group and vowed to one day become good enough to join it. The following summer I began taking classes with Frank Hatchett at the Broadway Dance Center. I took two to three beginning classes a day and was determined to become an eligible dancer. What I learned in Frank's class, however, went far beyond technique and a warm-up. I was given a gift not only as a performer, but as a human being.

I spent the first half of that summer's classes tucked away in the back of Studio A, way off in a corner, becoming visible only when the class was divided into groups and asked to do the combination. I will never forget the day Frank singled me out after my group danced the combination. He stopped the class, looked at me, and said, "Girl, you gotta put more flavor into that." Embarrassed, I tried to be clever and responded, "Sorry, but I'm afraid this is as tasty as I get." I cocked my head, jutted out a hip, and waited for the next truthful hint from the man I would one day refer to as "Papa." He stared at me, smiled, and said "Okay, Tasty B, let's see some of that attitude in your dancing. I want to see your individual style. I want to see your personal flavor. I want to see you." This unique "me" was a concept I couldn't relate to. I had not a clue *who* he was referring to.

As classes continued and I became more confident, I slowly crept my way up to the front lines. For the longest time, however, I could not bear to look at myself in the mirror. People had been staring at me all my life and telling me how I looked—my own true reflection never seemed really necessary. Well, I learned the hard way that "spotting" in dance is extremely important if one wants to learn how to turn. Soon after finding my place in the front row, I found myself on my butt on the floor after attempting a turn.

I wanted to cry and run out of the room. Frank was the reason I didn't. He came right over to me, helped me up, and said, "Don't sweat it kid, it happens to the best of dancers, but you better start looking at yourself in the mirror or you'll never be able to turn. How are you ever going to find your personal style if you don't know what you look like? Plus," he added, "everybody else is busy checking themselves out. You might as well do it too."

I had always assumed that it was arrogant and vain to look in the mirror. What would people think? Plus, what if I didn't like what I saw? Papa Frank insisted that if I didn't begin focusing on myself and what I individually could bring to each movement, I would never grow and be able to experience honest, creative expression. "Make it yours, Miss B." (I was Miss B when I was being given a life lesson!) "Give me attitude!" I also grew up believing attitude was a bad thing, an unattractive quality. However, I soon learned that it was the very essence that fuses the music with expression. Attitude is what makes the dance come alive and each movement individual.

Papa Frank became my mentor, and the subsequent school year I was not only promoted to the "dancer group," I was also accepted into a separate dance company.

Being in Frank's class gave me a sense of confidence, freedom, and inspiration I never had before. I came alive whenever the music was on. I found the "me" Frank was referring to. Studio A was my sanctuary, my arena free of judgment and full of possibility. It was the only place that remained constant for me. I could count on the fact that no matter what was happening in my life, I had a place to belong, a place that would allow me to explore and discover my personal style. In class I was included, yet unique.

Frank's combinations provided a metaphor for life and its ever-changing, eclectic nature. He always had the latest and hottest music and newest vibe. It was impossible not to groove, and when I realized that no two grooves were alike, it was quite liberating. His unique style runs the gamut in sensibility. VOP incorporates everything from lyrical to funk, from primal African and sensual Latin to raw hip-hop. VOP is a groove that combines technique and style infused with personal flavor. I used to fear technique because I lacked training, but Frank said that while technique without style lacked emotional content, style without the control, intrinsic to technique, lacked value.

My life changed the moment I walked into the back corner of Studio A. Dance has affected my life and career more than any other art form. It taught me self-expression and security. I would never have been able to perform eight shows a week on Broadway as Rizzo in *Grease,* nor would I ever have been offered the role of Roxy in *Chicago* on Broadway. My caricature was even added to the wall at the famed Sardi's restaurant because I performed in *Grease.* Even today the executive producers of *Suddenly Susan* add dancing whenever they can because they know I will be able to handle it. From the back of Studio A to center stage to the wall at Sardi's, I have been steadily moving forward.

People always ask me about Frank's style. It's hard to do it justice because along with great moves, he also teaches that our best is always better than we'd expect, and that there is no such thing as failure as long as the goal is to enjoy and grow.

Words can't fully express the feeling of freedom you get as Frank enthusiastically yells, "and five and six and ha-ha-ha!" or the celebration of oneself that his class provides. This book however, does give a terrific view of the man and his passion. It shines a light on Papa Frank and his commitment to his "kids," the art of dance, and the power of individual expression. Enjoy it and never stop dancing.
—Brooke Shields, actress, Star of *Suddenly Susan*

Preface

Through years of teaching, choreographing, and performing, Frank Hatchett has shared his unique style of jazz dance, known as *VOP*, with thousands of dancers. From Broadway to Paris, from Myrtle Beach to Tokyo, and from Hartford to Honolulu, students ask Frank the same question about his technique: "Will you please write it down so we can teach it?" It's easy to understand why. Jazz dance itself has become an icon of pop culture and the entertainment industry. The term *jazz dance* evokes images ranging from professional theater to music videos to fitness classes and dance recitals. Jazz dance is pervasive and embedded in our culture. As a leading driver of the innovation and energy of jazz dance, Frank Hatchett is recognized internationally as one of the legends of the jazz dance world. VOP, Frank Hatchett's unique style of jazz dance, is as complex as ballet but as embrace-able as MTV for today's generation.

I have studied dance with Frank Hatchett for 30 years. Together he and I have created this easy-to-use, information-rich, one-of-a-kind book, in which we share our winning approach for learning the Hatchett style. Our intention is to create both a learning and a teaching tool for the dancer, teacher, choreographer, and anyone else interested in jazz dance.

But what is VOP? VOP (rhymes with hop) is an exclamation that Frank started using early in his teaching career to help students accent a step or stylize a movement. He would encourage his dancers to respond energetically in jazz class by shouting, "5, 6, 7, 8, VOP!" VOP has since become synonymous with the Frank Hatchett style of jazz dance. Its energy, expressiveness, rhythmic freedom, and physical conditioning intrigue dancers and audiences alike.

The Hatchett style is also a performing art. It succeeds as an art form by combining technical ability, artistic interpretation, and a defining marriage between the music and the movement. Frank Hatchett's unique style encompasses the freedom, spirit, and beauty of jazz dance while promoting the emotional discovery and artistic interpretation of the dancer.

The book begins with an introduction to Frank Hatchett. We take you behind the scenes to get some background on the man. Frank is not only recognized as the creator of VOP, but also is loved, respected, and admired throughout the dance world.

The book is then divided into two parts. Part I defines the Hatchett style and helps you understand what it is and from where it came. Part I concludes with a powerful chapter entitled, "Spirit of the Dance," which allows you to take an inside look at VOP's defining attributes. Just as an artist's palette can make a canvas come alive, these attributes can create a vivid, inspiring experience not only for you as a dancer, but for your audience as well. We will teach you how. This insider's look will bring new focus to dancers at every level of technique.

Part II is for dancers at all skill levels who want to learn the Hatchett style. But before you can VOP, you have to warm up your body. The purpose of warming up is three-fold. First, it increases your flexibility and strength, reducing the risk of injury. Second, it nurtures the control necessary to develop technique. Finally, when done properly, the warm-ups get you in the groove to dance. Warm-ups include rhythmic, center, floor, and isolation exercises. Our easy-to-follow, step-by-step approach is supported by photographs of dancers doing the exercises.

Next, we get into the heart of the book . . . dancing. We've found over the years that the best way to teach the Hatchett style is based on a simple approach: Explore the style of movement, create combinations, and then reinforce the spirit of the dance. You will first learn to explore movements through basic, beginner, advanced beginner, and intermediate/advanced levels. We then give you the opportunity to create your own jazz movement, making up your own combinations or mini-experiences using all that you've learned. Next, we bring it together by reinforcing and intertwining the spirit of the dance and your own artistic interpretation to create VOP's unique flavor. The powerful energy and feeling that is created by applying these essentials is what Frank's style is all about.

In part II, the Hatchett Hints provide an additional benefit to the dancer or teacher. Hatchett Hints address proper alignment, technical training, and the most common areas for improvement that we have recognized over the years. In giving you the movements and explaining how to put it all together with VOP, we have addressed the "secrets" that make the style come alive.

So come join us. Lace up your jazz shoes and get ready to step up and VOP!

Acknowledgments

We extend our extreme appreciation to Dori Sullivan, who helped us tie everything together on tight schedules. We couldn't have done this without you. We love you!

Thanks go to Jason Warley, who posed for many of the photographs, and to our photographer Rick Stone.

Thanks to my colleagues at the YMCA, who were full of encouragement and support.

Thanks to my friends Michelle Wodarczyk, Susan Veine, and Lisa Longworth, who were always there for me.

We would like to thank Judy Patterson Wright and Cynthia McEntire of Human Kinetics for a world of insight, perspective, and guidance.

Who would have thought 30 some years ago that the cute little blonde girl in the black leotards doing cartwheels in the hallway at Tech High School would end up playing such a major part in carrying on the Hatchett legacy?

Nancy, I am so proud and grateful for this labor of love and your dedication to this project. Thank you from the bottom of my heart. Love, Papa Frank.

Thank you, Frank, for a world of knowledge and experience. I've been so fortunate to have you in my life. Not only have you been my guiding and loving "Papa Frank," but my inspiration as well. Love, Nancy.

The Man and His Magic

The magic behind the Hatchett style, known as VOP, is its emphasis on artistic interpretation. The interpretation requires a deliberate marriage between the music and the movement. "You must dig right down to your center and feel. Feel the movement and VOP the steps. Respond to the music from your soul, how it was originally intended, whether African, jazz, or hip-hop," says Frank. He continues, "At the core of jazz dance is the interpretation of the music. It is my obligation to the musician to express what he feels when he's playing. The interpretation all boils down to the relationship between the movement and the music." When done correctly, this relationship can create performance artistry.

The performance ability that comes from the VOP style is driven by Frank's creative process. His dancers become an integral part of the choreography and music. They are viewed as participants in the mutual creation of the dance, not just as programmed robots performing a mechanical reproduction. Students are encouraged to accent the movement with their own personal interpretation, while still holding onto Frank's style. Original thought and impressions are stressed in developing the choreographic and improvisational talents of his students. More so, these skills help to create the complete dancer.

As children and even as adults, we always saw Frank as a massive figure, both in stature and in deed. He has the ability to mesmerize a room before even taking a step. He has been a mentor, a friend, an inspiration, and a strong guiding force in our lives and dance careers.

Kim and Troy Norrington, studio owners

Whether in the classroom or on the dance convention circuit, Frank is full of encouragement, and the dancers sense his approval. His excitement and energy challenge students to work to their highest potential. In an environment of professionalism and mutual respect, students know to come prepared to dance; the expectation is to "get down to business" and learn. His signature marks of high energy and fun enable the learning process.

A positive approach to life is pervasive in his teaching style. "I love what I do," says Frank with strong conviction. "My students are here, and I know I have them from the minute they walk into class. They're not just hanging out. I feel they care about why they are here, and I want to teach them and to give them what they need." While the students spark his vitality, "it works both ways. Their intensity and need to learn inspire me. The chemistry between us is strong and special. I feel it and so do they."

Frank's classes at the Broadway Dance Center in New York City are an interesting mix. Professional and aspiring dancers, actors, actresses, singers, and models seeking to build a strong foundation in movement fill the studio. Many have gone on to successful careers in the entertainment field. Over the years, many famous people have studied with Frank: Brooke Shields, Madonna, Vanessa

Williams, Naomi Campbell, Olivia Newton-John, Justine Bateman, Savion Glover, MTV's Julie Brown, and dozens of Broadway and soap opera television actors and actresses. But Frank still maintains a large program for all levels, including children. His policy is one of inclusion.

For years Frank has provided a unique opportunity for his dancers, both professional and nonprofessional, to perform on stage. Frank presented the annual Broadway Dance Center showcase at Lincoln Center or another major venue in New York City. The showcase served as a learning opportunity for students. They practiced overcoming audition nerves and stage fright, and also got the opportunity to display their talents in dance, drama, singing, acting, and comedy. But to Frank, it doesn't matter if you are the next rising star or someone just reaching for a dream. The school is his extended family, the showcase his photo album. And in the process, Frank helps many people fulfill their dreams. As Frank tells a group of young dancers, "Reach for the moon, and if you don't make it you're still among the stars."

Frank has a desire to help his dancers. He has provided moral support to young dancers far from home who have come to New York City to study. His office at Broadway Dance Center is a second home for his students. They don't come just to socialize but also to talk candidly about their futures. One subject frequently discussed is auditions. For dancers, learning to cope with auditions and rejections is an important skill. Understanding this, Frank has created a nurturing environment. He explains, "I wanted to set up an atmosphere where [students] would feel welcome and accepted. A place to socialize, to discuss an upcoming audition, or to shed tears after being rejected from an audition. I teach them to learn from those experiences, to take an audition as they would a class, and to use it as a way of knowing what a particular choreographer expects from them next time."

Frank sees inside people and inspires them to bring out their potential. Frank teaches more than dance; he teaches about life.

Steven Boyd, teacher and choreographer

The Man

In Studio 3B at the Broadway Dance Center, Frank Hatchett, an impressive, exciting, and powerful man, tells the dancers the importance of making a memorable entrance and exit on stage. "When you step onstage, give the audience a sense of anticipation. And leave them with a groove. You're gone, but they're still feeling the vibrations," he commands. The overflowing class executes his directions.

The man knows how to make an entrance and leave a lasting impression. Loved and admired throughout the world for his unique style of jazz dance and inspirational teaching style, Frank Hatchett is quite simply one of the legendary jazz dance masters. His incredible classes for beginners through professionals are bonded by a unique energy and spirit.

So where did Frank and this enduring style come from? Born into a musical family, Frank was influenced early in life by his parents, Frank and Mary Hatchett. Family members sang gospel. His father played the piano professionally. His sister danced. As a child, one of Frank's chores was to take his sister to dance class weekly at Mary Morlock's studio in East Hartford, Connecticut. Frank typically passed the time waiting for his sister's class to end by reading comic books . . . or so it seemed. Little Frank was actually doing the steps in his head, visualizing himself in the classroom.

During one of his sister's scheduled dance classes, Mary was delayed due to a snowstorm. The girls remained, diligently practicing their tap. Little Frank watched his sister and the other young girls practice the steps. He became visibly frustrated and let the girls know they were not doing it correctly. Frank sprang up and demonstrated the steps just as a shocked Mary Morlock arrived. From then on, Mary encouraged Frank to participate in her classes. Before Frank was comfortable studying at Mary's studio, she had him study at her home. She placed wood planks on her mother's kitchen floor and gave Frank private lessons. He felt safe there; he didn't feel self-conscious. Mary worked on Frank, building his confidence, nurturing his expressiveness and dance ability. Morlock was Frank's first teacher, and Frank credits her as his inspiration. Frank credits Mary not only for encouraging him to dance but also for stimulating his dancer's spirit and feeling and nurturing the VOP within him. Mary eventually convinced Frank to join his sister in the studio's upcoming dance recital. It took his Aunt Dee's $1 tip to give Frank the extra encouragement he needed to participate. The audience's applause, combined with the energy and excitement of the performance, convinced Frank to pursue a career in dance.

Frank's dancing progressed quickly, and his teaching ability began to surface even as a teenager. Encouraged by his grandmother, Mamie Brandon, he started teaching friends in her basement. His friends were eager for Frank to show them the latest dance steps.

Frank continued his dance education at the University of Connecticut, but after one year he moved to Philadelphia to study with Eleanor Harris. Harris was a noted dancer, teacher, and choreographer as well as someone to whom talent scouts looked for upcoming talent. Harris scheduled an audition for Frank for a Las Vegas-style revue in Atlantic City called "Smart Affairs." He was hired and the show was a big success. After 12 weeks, the show moved to the Dunes hotel on the Las Vegas strip. During the time Frank was in Las Vegas, he underwent an experience that would refocus his life. One night after the show an elderly man introduced himself, then went on to congratulate him on the show's success and his performance. The man remarked on how much Frank reminded him of himself many years ago. He explained to Frank how he had toured Europe as a heralded young dancer. The man advised Frank to

> Frank has been blessed with the ability of taking a person's innermost feelings and having them brought forth and translated into movement that surpasses one's physical and mental reach, through sweat and tears.
>
> *Lane Napper, actor and choreographer*

"build some security; don't end up like me." Frank reflected for quite a while on this conversation. At first he was flattered, but then he realized that the man was the hotel's dishwasher. Concerned about his own future, Frank left the show shortly thereafter and returned to college.

After attending college, Frank purchased a storefront property in Springfield, Massachusetts, and converted it into a studio where students could come to study dance and also work on performances. In 1967 Frank received a teaching offer from the Dunbar Community Center in Springfield. His dance program quickly grew to become a major part of the center. The program became known as the Frank Hatchett Center for the Performing Arts and continued there until 1984. The school's registration grew to over 700 students and represented the future, stability, and accomplishment that Frank had been seeking.

Frank was just what the community needed. He showered the community with his appreciation for the arts and for his students. Jazz, African, tap, and ballet were just a few dance forms that were part of the curriculum. His mentoring caused him to become a father figure to many of his students and resulted in the nickname, "Papa Frank." He gave much of himself to his extended family of children, even demanding to see their school report cards. If their grades were not good, they weren't allowed to perform with the Hatchett Dancers, the school's performing company. He helped build his students' self-esteem and taught them about self-discipline. "Frank Hatchett was absolutely the best, a man who would do anything for a kid, a parent's dream come true. He helped more kids than you can count," says Warren Myers, supervisor of music in the Springfield Public School system.

Once the Frank Hatchett Center for Performing Arts was well established, Frank began to branch out, eager to explore other challenges. He formed the Frank Hatchett Trio with Wyetta Turner and Coco Dushon. The trio toured the United States and Europe. He began choreographing professionally in New York and became actively involved with many of the national dance conventions. He toured with Dance Makers, Dance Olympus, Dance Educators, Dance Masters, and many others, sharing his unique style of jazz dance.

In the early 1980s Frank relocated to New York and began teaching at several dance studios, including Jerry LeRoy's and Henry Le Tang. Sue Samuels invited him to join her and JoJo Smith at JoJo's Dance Factory. In 1982 Frank teamed up with Maurice Hines and renamed the studio Hines and Hatchett. Even-

tually Hines left, and Frank and Richard Ellner opened the Broadway Dance Center. They had a wide and inspiring vision of what the school could become. The Broadway Dance Center continues strong today, attracting top teachers and thousands of dancers from all over of the world to attend classes in any given week.

Frank has left a permanent impression on the world of dance. As one of the world's jazz dance masters, he is recognized and respected as a passionate innovator, visionary, and choreographer.

Part I

Frank Hatchett's VOP

CHAPTER 1

The Evolution of VOP

VOP /vop/

Noun: a unique energy put into dance as well as life; a spirit; a flavoring; a style; an attitude; a flair; a passion; a centeredness; a get-down, street-smart feeling; an individual interpretation of the music.

Verb: to communicate with an audience; to make the audience feel part of the dance experience.

VOP is synonymous with the Frank Hatchett style. VOP is not an acronym; nor do the letters "V" "O" "P" have any particular meaning. VOP originated as a way for Frank to urge his students to respond energetically to the music or to accent a step. It is the yell at the end of the "5, 6, 7, 8"count. It is pure inspiration to Frank's students. But on a deeper level, the Hatchett style is characterized by an artistic interpretation of music. Frank encourages dancers to connect with the music, creating a defining marriage between the music and movement. With Frank, music frequently leads creativity and development of the movement.

> At age 14 I took my first dance class with Frank. When class was over, no one wanted to leave. We could have danced all night. Frank truly changed my life by helping me discover what brought me the most happiness . . . dancing.
>
> *A.C. Ciulla, Tony-nominated choreographer, Broadway's* Footloose

Movements are not choreographed with disregard for the music. The music and movement complement one another, creating great combinations, choreography, and performances.

In addition to the music and movement, the essence of VOP comes from the dancer's soul. The dancer's creative inner self should be expressed and shared with the audience. The Hatchett style successfully fuses the dancer's expression of spirit, projection, attitude, energy, and rhythm. Brought together, these elements stylize the movement in a unique way. Frank instills the importance of individuality into his dancers. He brings out their own personalities and uniqueness. The result is far from cookie-cutter dancers. For instance, take a basic step touch movement. The movement is consistent across beginner jazz dance classes worldwide. Stylize the movement the Hatchett way, and the step touch takes on a whole new dimension. Because the Hatchett style reflects individual interpretation of music and the times, it is an everchanging style of jazz dance.

Individual interpretation, however, does not imply freestyle. VOP has a structured style and technique. Like other dance forms, it needs both discipline and dedication. One of VOP's challenges is to master its obvious contrast. The style appears supercharged and highly interpretative simultaneously. Supercharged dance shows strength, dynamics, rhythmic expressiveness, and explosive controlled energy. But simultaneously, the Hatchett style is highly interpretive. It can be perceived as soft, cool, artistic, and flowing. Making this contrast work is highly dependent on the dancer's technique. Through proper technique, the dancer maintains control and performs the movement cleanly. Technique also gives the dancer maturity and a solid foundation on which to successfully build more difficult technical movements.

> VOP is a must for any dancer who wants to move with attitude. Frank Hatchett is the man to give it to you.
>
> *Jacquie Bird*

But while technique is valued, concentrating solely on technique can constrain the dancer from feeling the music. The Hatchett style requires dancers to let go and free themselves. Once freed from concentrating solely on technique, the dancer can express and experience the feeling and fusion of the music and movement. Without this freedom the dancer will be too stiff, and the movements will appear as minor variations of jazz dance routines.

Just as a dancer must be able to let a movement go, he or she must know when and how to stay in control of the movement. This brings us back to proper technique. For instance, when thrusting a leg through a grand battement, you need to have the energy and strength to lift your leg. You also need to stay in control so you don't hop all over the place to get to the next movement. Even if the movement calls for you to have a lot of energy, it shouldn't look as though you're out of control.

VOP remains a unique form of jazz dance, reflecting individual interpretation of the music, the times, and the dancer. So free yourself and let go. Feel the music. Experience the fusion. Perform with fluidity, smooth transitions, and control, which are necessary in developing the Hatchett style.

Where Did VOP Come From?

Dance training, music, culture, the rhythm of life—these factors all contributed to the development of the Hatchett style. They are at the heart of VOP's origin. As you will learn, the Hatchett style didn't start at the Broadway Dance Center in New York City. Frank Hatchett and his unique style of jazz dance evolved from many influences.

Early in Frank's career, his teachers tried to make him conform to their techniques. He complied, but inside he yearned for greater individual interpretation and expression through dance. As Frank matured and transitioned to the role of teacher and choreographer, he seized the opportunity to incorporate other dance styles and influences to create the style he wanted. The result was an exciting, expressive dance form. In the remainder of this chapter, we learn about the influences in Frank's life that helped to create the Hatchett style.

Teachers

Katherine Dunham was one of the major influences on Frank and his style. Katherine Dunham brought the richness of the African-American heritage to dance by popularizing the use of folklore, ritualistic, and ethnic dancing. Frank recalls how Dunham combined tribal movements from Africa with modern dance. The fluidity of Dunham's movements and choreography was her signature and became an inspiration to dancers. Today she is acknowledged as one of the founders of the anthropological dance movement. Sevilla Forte, Dunham's protégé, taught Frank at Phillips and Forte School of Dance in New York City when he was in his late teens. Forte is remembered as one of the best teachers Frank ever had. According to Frank, "She had a touch that would correct your body placement. Sevilla could establish your technique. Sevilla's influence and the Dunham foundation showed me how the body could be liberated from the rigidity of traditional technique to convey a powerful message without sacrificing technique."

African Dance

African dance was also influential. Its roots are based in the richness of cultural ceremonies that celebrate significant religious, community, or family events, such as courtship, marriage, harvest, and holidays. Frequently the dances were choreographed to reenact a

Traditional African movements and rhythms influenced VOP's energy.

story. Almost always, authentic African music was used to help translate these stories. The music and movement, when well integrated, provide a visual tapestry that has kept alive the cultural traditions of Africa for centuries.

When Frank started teaching, African movements, challenging rhythms, and proper technique influenced his style. Frank would stimulate his students' interest in African dance by having them dance in traditional African style, barefoot and accompanied by a live percussion ensemble known as the Aruhu Drummers. This teaching method resulted in dramatic movements, improvisational freedom, and synchronized group movements. Frank incorporated more of a Western attitude, melding the authentic African movements and music with contemporary influences.

East Indian Dance

Frank loved East Indian dances because they used many different qualities simultaneously. Similar to the movements of African dance, East Indian dance incorporates subtle differences such as facial attitudes and expressive use of the dancers' hands. For instance, East Indian dancers traditionally tell stories with their hands (see photo on p. 6). By incorporating this element into his choreography, Frank enhanced the dancers' overall expressiveness.

Caribbean Dance

Growing up in East Hartford exposed the young Frank Hatchett to many other dance influences. On Saturday afternoons, Frank frequently went to see MGM musicals at the local movie theater. He enjoyed the choreography of these musicals, especially the Caribbean numbers.

Years later while studying the Dunham style, Frank understood how musical theater choreography was influenced by traditional Caribbean and Calypso folk dance. These dances were influenced by the history, music, traditions, and folklore of the Caribbean people. Frank also recognized Spanish and

The visual storytelling of East Indian dancing inspired the unique expressiveness of VOP.

African influences in Caribbean dance. The Calypso style, for instance, requires freedom of movement while maintaining control. Calypso movements emphasize the torso, specifically the back and pelvis. The Calypso beat draws upon counterpoint rhythms such as those found in Flamenco dance. Frank loved the freedom of movement and used Caribbean style music to extract attitude and feeling from his dancers. He would incorporate the Caribbean and Calypso rhythms into classes to encourage expression and individual interpretation. This gave him a chance to learn about the dancers' range of abilities.

Martial Arts

Turning to the far East, Frank was influenced by the strength, power, and focus of the martial arts. He liked the intensity and the way the movements required changing focus quickly without losing concentration and control. Later, we cover how to use focus and direction of a movement to execute smoother transitions.

Hip-Hop

The music and rhythms of hip-hop are rooted in the drums of Africa and the streets of America. The original hip-hop dancers were known as street dancers. Street dancers were frequently urban youths who displayed their talents in public. Rather than trying to gain respect through violence, street dancers earned respect by showing off their art. Some of hip-hop's original movements included popping, locking, and breaking. Hip-hop shares many characteristics of the improvisational qualities of jazz dance, for instance, letting the feeling, spirit, and music take over while dancing.

In the 1970s Frank incorporated basic hip-hop movements in the classroom. He eventually was recognized as one of the first jazz dance teachers to incorporate this dance style. He has used hip-hop as an inspiration for creating movements. Hip-hop's technique and vocabulary are different from other dance forms, but hip-hop should be appreciated for its nuances and innovation. The style's commercial success has influenced everything from jazz dance to clothing to aerobics.

The Rhythm of Life

A key contributor to Frank's style is his awareness of the rhythm of life. Frank has developed the keen ability to internalize the rhythm around him. When he hears a sound—for example, a dripping faucet, a whirring fan, traffic on a busy street—he finds beauty in its rhythm. He then duplicates it in his dance. To see how he does this, try visualizing a construction site. The machines are at work. Imagine the tapping and vibration of drills and jackhammers. Let the sounds you might hear begin to generate rhythms and movements in your mind. Another example is to imagine yourself running a hand through your wet hair, then flicking the water off your fingertips. Such ordinary experiences can be incorporated into rhythm and give movement its own flavor and style. The rhythm of life can be seen in Frank's choreography today.

A great example of how Frank incorporated everyday experiences into his style is the story behind the Attitude Walk, one of Frank's signature moves. Miss Flossy, Frank's neighbor when he was a young boy, inspired the move. Miss Flossy was an older woman. During the week, she wore an apron, but on Sundays she stepped out dressed like a queen. Miss Flossy had a walk that matched her clothes, a walk loaded with attitude that evoked fierce confidence. Young Frank watched Miss Flossy and her distinctive walk. Later in life, Frank took this memory and used it to develop the Attitude Walk.

Each of these experiences contributed to the Hatchett style and added a significant technical, artistic, or rhythmic influence.

CHAPTER 2

The Spirit of the Dance

The more you relax, the more you let go.

The more you let go, the more you get down.

The more you get down, the more you feel it.

The more you feel it, the more you project.

The more you project, the more you give attitude.

The more you give attitude, the more you energize.

The more you energize, the more you feel the music.

The more you feel the music, the more you VOP.

–Nancy Myers Gitlin

This verse summarizes the building blocks of the Hatchett style. In this chapter, we'll explain how VOP's essential elements fuse together to form the essence of the Hatchett style. We'll show you how these elements work together and complement each other. Together they achieve the special flavor and style that sets apart this jazz dance form. These elements are, simply, the spirit of the dance.

In this chapter, we will break down the elements of projection, focus, attitude, energy, music, flavor, and fusion. Each element will be explained, and we'll share how it relates to movement and the audience. This will give

you a better understanding of what the Hatchett style is all about. You'll see that it takes more than just mastering the movements. Each element is critical, equally important on its own but also interdependent. The final element, fusion, is what brings VOP to life and makes it happen. Now get ready to catch and feel the spirit of the dance.

Projection Communicates

Projection is the dancer's ability to communicate personality, dynamics, and empathy to the audience. It's a feeling from within, an

Project the spirit of the dance to the back row of the audience.

Dancers need to get comfortable with the space around them. Space yourselves so that everyone can do the combination without being cramped; in other words, "let the floor breathe."

Focus helps you achieve proper alignment and, therefore, makes it easier to learn new movements. For example, if you are supposed to look to the side, don't focus in the mirror. Focusing sideways will automatically help adjust your alignment. You'll soon discover that most movements have focus, whether you are focusing front, back, side, up, down, or to the corner.

Attitude Counts

Attitude is about carrying off a movement with commitment, personality, style, confidence, and self esteem. Attitude is a sense of security or mood conveyed through self-expression.

The dancer should own the floor. Strike, step, and hit the pose with confidence. But don't just hit a position; move with feeling. Attitude is about strutting your stuff, not slinking along as though you're walking to the laundromat. Try tossing a look over your shoulders or flicking your hand with feeling. But to capture your audience, make your facial expressions natural, not forced.

inner self-expressiveness generated outward. It's the way you feel from the heart, the want, the desire, and the love for the art. Once achieved, it's projected outward. Projection is what the audience sees.

Successful projection makes your audience emotionally get involved in your performance. It's key to remember that different feeling and intensity levels are associated with projection. The variations of moods are infinite. The levels of projection are equally broad. Make sure you don't project only to the front row of your audience. Even if the projection is subtle, the audience should feel it all the way in the back row. Projection enhances the whole stage. Practice projection by splitting into groups and performing for each other. Work on eye contact and natural facial expressions.

Frank's personality is bigger than any room in which he has taught. He energizes the dancers, teachers, parents, and even those observing. He gives of himself, never asking in return. He is a teacher in the true sense of the word.

Bill Hotaling, Director, Manhattan Dance Project

If you've never applied attitude before, try a basic visualization technique. Just as championship athletes often imagine their moment of truth, so can you. Picture yourself being sassy, cutesy, confident, or whatever the mood of the dance calls for. Then apply this image to your attitude within the movement.

Learning to release your inhibitions will also help you develop attitude. It's natural to feel inhibited, awkward, or uncomfortable at first. Be persistent. Attitude develops over time. It starts by becoming comfortable with

Focus Directs

Focus is about maintaining mental concentration and understanding where you are going.

the movements and your environment, then leads to feeling the movements with confidence. Attitude ultimately becomes the frosting on a cake that provides the finishing touch.

You can practice giving attitude in front of a mirror or by watching each other. This approach will let you see and feel the attitude. It's important to recognize that everyone develops attitude at his or her own pace. Although it's good to watch others in class, it's okay if you don't look just like them. Try to discover your own attitude instead of copying someone else's. Keep in mind that we are referring to attitude here, not technique. The technique cannot be compromised. Allow yourself to individualize your attitude and develop your own personality.

Energy Motivates

Energy is the power, force, and aura a dancer puts into movement. It brings the movement to life and enhances your projection.

Varying the energy of the movement will help you become more versatile. It can be strong and powerful, smooth and soft, or sharp and crisp. Just like music's crescendos and accents, you can infuse movement with multiple levels of energy to affect the audience's impression.

Energy must always be controlled. Too much energy leads to wild, uncontrolled movements. The dancer's centeredness is lost. Control therefore is critical. For instance, you may perform a high kick into a layout with an intense burst of energy, but then you will need to make a smooth transition into the next movement. The movements should appear placed and smooth, not sloppy or choppy. Strive to make all your movements look clean.

Energy enhances the overall performance. From energy, the spirit of the dancer shines. The spirit helps make the performing experience incredibly satisfying and exciting not only to you but to the audience as well. If you shuffle to the stage flat-footed, the audience will think hurry up and get it over with. When you enter, give them a sense of anticipation and leave them with a groove. You're gone, but they're still feeling the vibration. Energy generates audience participation. When the audience gets going, they'll want to get up and move with you (sometimes they actually do!).

Music Matters

The roots of jazz dance are grounded in jazz music. The essence is in the interpretation. The interpretation by the dancer or the choreographer is the overall complement to the music.

In class, Frank teaches more than dance. He teaches each student what timing is all about and how to feel the music. The dancer must have the discipline to be on the right count of the music. Listen and respond to the music, then capture the spirit of the piece. The movement must fit the rhythm, phrasing, mood, and dynamics of the music.

Ultimately a marriage must occur between the music and the movement. You can't have the music on one planet and the movement on another. Don't just do the steps—feel the music.

Select music that is interesting and inspirational. Music is the driving force for creativity. The music should stimulate your mind and enhance the projection, attitude, and energy. For Frank, a certain mood of the music or accent or beat inspires him to create something brand new.

Frank believes that it's our obligation to respect the compositions of musicians. Try imagining what the composer or musician was feeling when he or she created the music. Then try to incorporate the movements with the music. Prechoreographing, that is, creating movement and then selecting music, is not suggested. By embracing the music we reach out for what the composer was thinking. For instance, will all the crescendos and accents tie together when you start staging this? Music without accents can be boring for everyone, especially the audience. Listen to your music for dynamics, rhythm changes, and mood changes. Use them to your advantage, enhancing your choreography and creativity.

Syncopation is a useful tool in creating different rhythms. This can be achieved by emphasicing an "&" count before a beat. If your movement is all on strong beats (1, 2, 3, 4, 5, 6, 7, 8), then add the "&" count to create syncopation. For example:

&1, &2, 3, 4, &5, &6, 7, 8

1, 2, 3, &4, 5, 6, 7, &8

1, 2, &3, 4, 5, 6, &7, 8

1, 2, &3, 4, 5, &6, 7, 8

The use of all "&" counts (&1, &2, &3, &4, &5, &6, &7, &8) is not considered syncopation in the Hatchett style.

If you ever have the chance to use live musicians in your class, such as drummers, do so. Frank uses live music from time to time to enhance the spirit, feeling, and overall dancing of his students. It's an incredible feeling to dance to live rather than canned music. It takes a little extra planning but is well worth it.

> VOP is used all over the world by many teachers, students, and performers. Frank has a unique way of creating his choreography. He is always helping students in every way possible. Frank has touched so many.
>
> *Grace Wakefield, Executive National Director, Starpower, Dancepower*

Vocalizing sounds is a great tool for digging deep within, so you feel the accents, rhythm, timing, and quality of the music. Vocalizing sounds involves making rhythms with the voice instead of counting. Make sure the sounds fit the movement, for example, "zaa baa aah aah," "boom boom ba," "chicka chicka boom," "pa de boo hoo [pas de bourrée]," "chaîné ne [chaîné]," "batte ma ma [battement]."

Flavor Enhances

Frank encourages dancers to accent, or flavor, the step with their own personal styles while holding onto his style. He also tries to get dancers to infuse a lively, positive energy not just in dance but also in life. He tells them to try to make a favorable, lasting impression whether they are auditioning or meeting new people, or even working in a non-dance environment.

Fusion Connects

Fusion is the magical integration of all the elements of the Hatchett style. It involves blending the projection, attitude, energy, and music to create the Hatchett style. Fusion is what VOP and Frank Hatchett are all about.

Sometimes a dancer executes a movement perfectly then just jumps into the next move without fusing them together—no transition whatsoever. The movements are not connected; the transitions are clumsy. Movements are not isolated, independent from one another. They should appear fluid and continuous. Don't stop between each movement; let the transitions flow. To illustrate this, try visualizing movements as sentences:

You

talk

If you can, use live drummers in your class.

in

sentences,

not

one

word

at

a

time.

This makes a lot more sense when fused together:

"You talk in sentences, not one word at a time."

Likewise, in dance, if we move one count at a time the dance will look and feel as choppy as our example.

Now that you understand the basic elements of the Hatchett style, you're ready for part II, where you will learn VOP style movements and how to put them all together with the spirit of the dance.

The next chapter, "Ready, Set . . . Warm Up!" introduces rhythmic, stretching, and isolation exercises. These exercises prepare the body to dance by increasing flexibility, developing technique, and improving coordination.

Let's start to dance. Come and get some VOP!

Part II

5, 6, 7, 8, VOP!

CHAPTER 3

Ready, Set . . . Warm Up!

> Frank taught me how to get a whole room full of students, of all different levels, in control and teach them a routine that's challenging and fun. I also learned the art of mentoring and inspiring teachers and students by speaking from my heart. Frank is unique, full of surprises, a wealth of information, and a loving "papa." —*Sheila Barker, teacher and choreographer*

This chapter focuses on preparing your body to dance. Warm-ups, isolations, and their proper use are detailed.

The primary purpose of warm-ups is to prepare the musculoskeletal system for activity.

Exercises are given to increase the flexibility, strength, and control necessary for developing proper technique. Good alignment and form not only help develop technique but also reduce the risk of injury. When muscles are warm the risk of injury decreases, range of motion increases, and muscle soreness is reduced. A second benefit of warm-ups is to help get you in the groove and motivated to dance. Set the tone by having a good attitude and using music that appeals to you. Effective music will increase energy, concentration, and attitude and provide inspiration. Use the warm-ups to get focused, disciplined, and always give 100 percent.

Warm Up Your Body to Dance

The four warm-up sections that follow are targeted to all dance levels. Rhythmic, center, floor, and isolation exercises are included. Rhythmic exercises help the dancer "get in the groove" and warm up the muscles before they are stretched. Always start with rhythmic exercises to gradually raise your body temperature. This will increase flexibility and decrease the risk of injury when warming up.

The center and floor stretch exercises increase strength, flexibility, and technique. Avoid bouncing (ballistic stretching) or rocking when stretching. Such movement increases muscle tension or contraction which leads to the risk of injury. Instead, hold the stretch and focus on slowly exhaling as you move into it more deeply. Do not exceed your own limitations. Never pull your leg farther than it will go naturally. Each exercise varies your requirements on holding a stretch and range anywhere from 10 seconds to 1 minute in length. Counting in half time helps sustain the stretch longer. To do this, count out one beat for every two beats.

Always follow the warm-ups with isolations. Isolation exercises warm up specific body parts and improve coordination. Isolations are done in a very precise manner and are critical to the Hatchett style. They add sharpness and fluidity to specific movements. Isolation work also helps you develop the ability to execute more challenging rhythmic movements. This allows you to move different body parts simultaneously with different rhythms while remaining in control.

> Frank Hatchett is philanthropic. He is such an inspiration and is always full of encouragement. The experiences we gained from Frank will stay with us forever.
>
> *The Williams Brothers, song and tap dance act*

As you learn the warm-ups, concentrate on proper alignment and technique. Through practice, technique will become automatic. As your technique grows, challenge yourself. Increase the difficulty of the exercise, but be careful not to sacrifice proper technique or to develop bad habits along the way.

The warm-up exercises are listed in an easy-to-follow, recommended sequence. You can also pick and choose exercises. Just be careful not to do a standing exercise followed by a floor exercise followed by a standing exercise. Switching from floor to standing makes transitions choppy. The objective here should be fluidity. We recommend performing all the warm-ups. When first learning or if time is limited, select five exercises from the rhythmic section, three exercises from the center stretch section, four exercises from the floor stretch section and all the body-part isolations (focus and traveling isolations are optional).

Beginners and advanced beginners should start by warming up for 20 minutes during a 1-hour class, gradually increasing the warm-up time to 30 minutes. It is normal to feel sore when learning new warm-ups. Over time your strength and flexibility will improve. Intermediate to advanced dancers should warm up for 45 minutes during a 1-hour and 30-minute class or 30 minutes for a 1-hour class. Even if you've danced for years, learning new warm-ups can work muscles you may not have worked much before. Once the exercises are learned, move from one to the next without stopping. This creates continuity and fluidity of movement and avoids muscles growing cold.

Breakdown of Warm-Up Exercises

Exercises are specified for all skill levels. Level designations are only an estimate, so use your own discretion. Each exercise identifies the muscles being stretched and strengthened. Understanding the basics of anatomy maximizes the benefits of each exercise and increases your knowledge of the body. Figures 3.1 and 3.2 show the major muscle groups and areas of the body used in the warm-up exercises.

For each exercise, we document the starting position, counts, movement, arms, Hatchett hints, and photographs to ensure that the warm-ups are of value and executed correctly. It is important to read the starting position first and the Hatchett hints throughout. If you're not in the proper position to start it can be more difficult to understand the exercises. The Hatchett hints provide tips for developing alignment and technique. Also included in each exercise are trigger words (part A, B, etc.) or teaching cues to help the dancer remember the exercise.

So, put on some music and get ready, set . . . warm up!

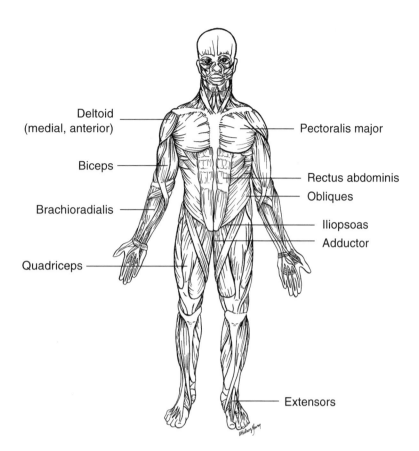

Figure 3.1 Muscle structure: front.

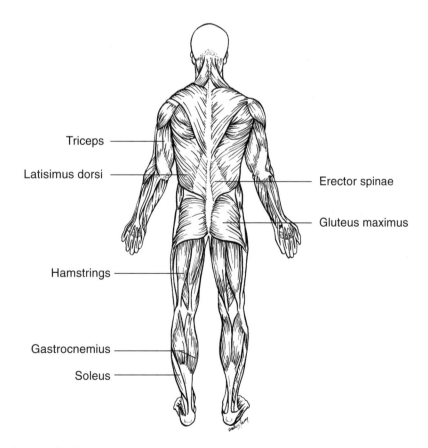

Figure 3.2 Muscle structure: back.

Beat to Beat: Rhythmic Exercises to Get In the Groove

Center Exercises

#	Warm-up	Skill level	Page number
1	Torso Side Reach	All	21
2	Contract n' Release	All	22
3	Plié Presses	All	23
4	Press n' Lift	All	25
5	Jazz Stance Press	All	26
6	Alternating Shoulder Press	All	27
7	Body Roll	Int/Advanced	28
8	Pliés in First	Int/Advanced	29

Warm-Up #1   Torso Side Reach

Skill level: All
Stretching: Side of torso (obliques)
Strengthening: Side of torso (obliques)
Starting position: Stand in second position turned out with straight legs; relax arms by sides.

Count	Movement	Arms

Part A: Lift head back, lower down.

1-2 Lift head back.
Press shoulders down.

3-4 Lower head down.
Lower chin toward chest.

Repeat part A 3 times.

Part B: Circle head R-L.

1-8 Circle head R ending R.

1-8 Circle head L ending L.

Repeat part B.

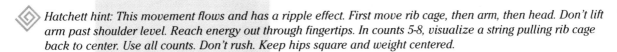

Hatchett hint: Lengthen neck as head circles back.

Part C: Rib reach R and back to center.

1-4 Move rib cage R.   Lift R arm side.
Tilt head R (see photo).

5-8 Move rib cage center.   Lower R arm down.
Move head center.

Repeat part C on L side.
Reduce part C using 2 counts for each movement. Perform 2 times on both sides.
Reduce part C using 1 count for each movement. Perform 4 times on both sides.

Hatchett hint: This movement flows and has a ripple effect. First move rib cage, then arm, then head. Don't lift arm past shoulder level. Reach energy out through fingertips. In counts 5-8, visualize a string pulling rib cage back to center. Use all counts. Don't rush. Keep hips square and weight centered.

Warm-Up #2   Contract n' Release

Skill level:	All
Stretching:	Back (erector spinae group); chest (pectoralis major)
Strengthening:	Back (erector spinae group)
Starting position:	Stand in second position parallel with straight legs; relax arms by sides

Count	Movement	Arms

Arms in second, contract, release, arms down.

Count	Movement	Arms
1-2		Lift arms side (photo a).
3-4	Contract torso back. Bend knees (photo b).	Move arms front.
5-6	Release torso front. Straighten legs (photo c).	Move arms back.
7-8	Move torso center.	Lower arms.

Repeat entire exercise 3 times.
Reduce entire exercise 2 times, using 1 count for each movement.

Hatchett hint: When moving arms front, lead arms with heels of hands. Chest stays lifted. When moving arms back, pull arms back from wrists.

a

b

c

22

Skill level: All
Stretching: Below the calf (soleus)
Strengthening: Top of thigh (quadriceps)
Starting position: Stand in first position parallel with straight legs; relax arms by sides.

Count	Movement	Arms

Part A: Press knees.

1-8 Press knees 8 times
(photo a).

 Hatchett hint: Don't overdo the knee press. Make sure heels stay on the floor. Press to the beat of the music to get you in the groove and develop better timing and rhythm. Keep torso straight but not stiff.

Part B: Press knees in first position turned out.

1-8 Rotate legs to first position.   Round arms down.
Press knees 8 times
(photo b).

 Hatchett hint: Place weight on heels. Don't let knees roll in. Lift elbows to round the arms.

Part C: Press knees in parallel second position.

1-8 Rotate legs out to parallel   Lift arms side (photo c).
second position.
Press knees 8 times.

 Hatchett hint: Place weight over balls of feet.

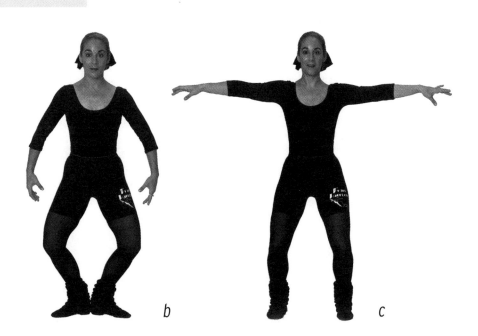

a   *b*   *c*

Part D: Press knees in second position turned out.

1-8	Rotate legs out to second position and press knees 8 times (photo d).	Round arms side.

 Hatchett hint: Place weight on heels. Lift elbows to round arms.

Part E: Press knees in parallel second position.

1-8	Rotate legs to parallel second with heels apart and press knees 8 times.	Straighten arms side.

 Hatchett hint: Turn palms down.

Part F: Press knees in turned-out first.

1-8	Rotate legs into first with heels together and press knees 8 times.	Round arms down.

Part G: Press knees in parallel first.

1-8	Rotate legs to parallel first and press knees 8 times.	Relax arms.

d

Skill level: All
Stretching: Calf (gastrocnemius); underside of thigh (hamstrings)
Strengthening: Top of thigh (quadriceps)
Starting position: Stand in first position parallel with bent knees; relax arms by sides.

Count	Movement	Arms

Part A: Slap thighs, reach up, lower down.

Count	Movement	Arms
1-3	Lean torso forward. Press knees 3 times (photo a).	Slap hands on sides of thighs 3 times.
&	Lean torso to flat back. Straighten legs with flexed feet. Place weight on heels (photo b).	Reach arms overhead.
4	Bend knees. Return toes to floor.	Relax arms down.

Repeat part A.

◇ *Hatchett hint: Relax and feel the music. Torso is relaxed. When reaching arms, with energy going through fingertips. Focus (look) down to floor.*

Part B: Slap thighs, rotate R, down center.

Count	Movement	Arms
1-3	Lean torso forward. Press knees 3 times.	Slap hands on thighs 3 times.
&	Lift torso up. Keep weight center. Rotate R leg out with R leg straight. Flex foot.	Clap hands once in front of chest.
4	Rotate R leg front with toes down. Bend R knee.	Relax arms down.

Repeat part B on L side.
Repeat part B on both sides.

Part C: Slap thighs, rotate R, down center.

Count	Movement	Arms
1-3	Lean torso forward. Press knees 3 times.	Slap hands on sides of thighs 3 times.
&	Rotate legs R, weight center. Flex R foot; lift L heel. Rotate torso R (photo c).	Bend R arm side. Lift L arm side; flex wrist.
4	Rotate torso and legs front. Bend knees.	Relax arms down.

Repeat part C on L side.
Repeat part C on both sides.

◇ *Hatchett hint: When rotating legs, rotate from hips, not knees.*

a

b

c

25

Skill level:	All	
Stretching:	Hip flexors (iliopsoas)	
Strengthening:	Top of thigh (quadriceps); side of shoulder (medial deltoid); stomach (rectus abdominus)	
Starting position:	Stand in second position turned out with straight legs; reach arms side; spread fingers (jazz hands); face palms front.	

Count	Movement	Arms

Part A: Press knees.

| **1-8** | Press knees 8 times (photo a). | |

◇ *Hatchett hint: Arms are strong with energy continuing through fingertips. Don't let arms move. Lift chest.*

Part B: Rotate R leg in and press knees.

| **1-8** | Rotate R leg in and lift heel (photo b). Press knees 8 times. | |

◇ *Hatchett hint: Keep weight centered. Rotate R leg from hip. Shoulders are square.*

Part C: Rotate R leg out and press knees.

| **1-8** | Rotate R leg out and lower heel. Press knees 8 times. | |

Repeat parts B and C on L.
Repeat entire exercise.

◇ *Hatchett hint: Keep ball of foot on floor.*

a

b

Warm-Up #6   Alternating Shoulder Press

Skill level:	All
Stretching:	Front of shoulder (anterior deltoid); inner thigh (adductors)
Strengthening:	Top of thigh (quadriceps)
Starting position:	Stand in second position slightly turned out with bent knees; place hands on tops of thighs with fingers facing in.

Count	Movement	Arms

Press shoulders R-L.

1-2	Lean torso to flat back (see photo).	Press R shoulder forward.
3-4		Press L shoulder forward; move R shoulder back.

Repeat entire exercise.
Reduce entire exercise 8 times using 1 count for each shoulder press.

 Hatchett hint: For counts 1-2, maintain a flat back to make it easier to press shoulder front. Keep hips square with weight centered. Don't let R knee move in.

Warm-Up #7   Body Roll

Skill level:	Intermediate/advanced
Stretching:	Chest (pectoralis major)
Strengthening:	Back (erector spinae group)
Starting position:	Stand facing R side; bend R knee in parallel position; bend L knee back in parallel position and lift heel; relax arms by sides.

Count	Movement	Arms
	Body roll; visualize a wall.	
&	Round torso forward to hip level.	Round arms down. Lift elbows.
1	Push head toward wall with L leg (photo a). Lift and brush forehead against wall.	
2	Continue lifting head. Brush chest against wall. Straighten legs and lift L heel.	
3	Brush pelvis against wall.	
4	Shift weight back (photo b). Bend knees and lift R heel.	

Repeat entire exercise.
Repeat entire exercise on R side 2 times.

Hatchett hint: Using a wall or visualizing one is an excellent tool to help you understand the feeling and flow of the movement. Back arches naturally. Motion of torso will be easier to execute if you remain aware of proper bending and straightening of legs.

a

b

Warm-Up #8   Pliés in First

Skill level:	Intermediate/advanced
Stretching:	Underside of thigh (hamstrings)
Strengthening:	Back (erector spinae group); stomach (rectus abdominus); top of thigh (quadriceps)
Starting position:	Stand in first position turned out with straight legs; round arms by sides.

Count	Movement	Arms
Part A: Demi-plié, straighten.		
1-2	Demi-plié.	Lift R arm side.
3-4	Straighten legs.	Lower R arm down.
	Repeat part A on L side.	

 Hatchett hint: Don't rush. Use all counts. Keep arms fluid and tighten stomach muscles throughout exercise.

Count	Movement	Arms
Part B: Grande plié, straighten halfway, coupé turn.		
1-5	Grand plié (photo a).	Lift R arm front and lift L arm side.
6	Straighten legs halfway.	
7-8	Coupé turn R (photo b).	Move L arm front.
	Press R knee out.	

 Hatchett hint: Keep chest lifted and legs turned out. Place knees over toes at bottom of grand plié. Don't let the knees roll in. On the coupé turn, keep R foot attached to L leg; press R knee out.

a

b

Part C: Plié L, passé R, straighten R leg front.

1-2	Plié L leg. Hold coupé R position.	Lower arms.
3-4	Passé R leg turned out. Press R knee side.	Lift arms front (photo c).
5-8	Straighten R leg front.	Lift L arm overhead. Open R arm side.

c

 Hatchett hint: For the passé, press R knee side. Stay lifted in L supporting leg. Hips remain square. For counts 5-8, chest is lifted with energy continuing through R foot and arms.

Part D: Relevé L, chassé front, battement L.

1-4	Relevé L leg.	
	(chassé front)	
5&6	Step R foot front. Step L foot forward behind R foot. Step R foot front.	Open L arm side.
7-8	Battement L leg. Step L foot front.	

 Hatchett hint: For the battement, keep arms in second and don't allow them to move up and down. Press shoulders down.

Part E: Battement R-L, pas de bourrée turn R, step to first.

1-2	Battement R leg. Step R foot front.	Arms in second.
3-4	Battement L leg. Step L foot front.	
5&6	Pas de bourrée turn R.	Lower arms.
7-8	Step L foot side. Step R foot to first position turned out.	

Repeat entire exercise on L side.

 Hatchett hint: For the pas de bourrée, use both counts to lower arms.

Muscle to Muscle: Stretching Exercises to Increase Flexibility

Center Exercises

#	Warm-up	Skill level	Page number
9	Release n' Stretch	All	32
10	Plié n' Stretch	Int/Advanced	34
11	Runner's Stretch	All	36

Floor Exercises

#	Warm-up	Skill level	Page number
12	Contract n' Flex	Int/Advanced	39
13	Reach n' Press	All	41
14	Hamstring Stretch	All	42
15	Changements	Int/Advanced	44
16	Straddle Stretch	All	45
17	Battements	All	48
18	Battement n' Stretch	Int/Advanced	49

Warm-Up #9   Release n' Stretch

Skill level: All
Stretching: Underside of thigh (hamstrings)
Strengthening: Back (erector spinae group); arms (when used as resistance)
Starting position: Stand in second position parallel with straight legs; relax arms by sides.

Count	Movement	Arms

Part A: Release down, roll up.

| 1-8 | Release torso down. Bend knees (photo a). | Round arms back. Lift elbows. |
| 1-8 | Roll torso up. Straighten legs. | Relax arms. |

Reduce part A using 4 counts for each movement. Repeat 2 times.

 Hatchett hint: Lead torso down with chest. Stretch buttocks upwards. Don't lower them toward knees. Roll torso up from bottom of spine, vertebrae by vertebrae. Head, shoulders, and arms fall naturally into place. Don't hold legs for support when rolling up. Use all counts. Don't rush.

Part B: Release down, stretch legs.

| 1-4 | Release torso down. Bend knees. | Round arms back. Lift elbows. |
| 5-8 | Straighten and stretch legs. Stretch torso toward legs (photo b). | Hold ankles. |

 Hatchett hint: While releasing torso, relax head—no tension. Place weight over balls of feet not over heels. You will develop better balance and flexibility. Use arms for added resistance to stretch torso down between legs.

a

b

Part C: Demi-plié, straighten.

1-4	Bend knees (photo c).
5-8	Straighten and stretch legs. Stretch torso between legs.

Repeat part C.

 Hatchett hint: For the demi-plié, keep heels on floor and buttocks stretching up. Don't lower buttocks to knees.

Part D: Demi-plié and flat back, straighten.

1-4	Stretch torso to flat back. Bend knees (photo d).
5-8	Straighten and stretch legs. Stretch torso between legs.

Repeat part D.

 Hatchett hint: For the flat back, lengthen neck; don't allow head to drop.

Part E: Roll up.

1-8	Roll torso up. Straighten legs.	Relax arms.

 Hatchett hint: Roll up from bottom of spine.

c

d

Skill level: Intermediate/advanced
Stretching: Side of torso (obliques); underside of thigh (hamstrings); back (erector spinae group)
Strengthening: Back (erector spinae group); arms (when used as resistance)
Starting position: Stand in second position turned out with straight legs; relax arms by sides.

Count	Movement	Arms

Part A: L arm in second, lean R.

| 1-4 | | Lift L arm side.
Round R arm (photo a). |
| 5-8 | Stretch torso R (photo b). | Reach L arm overhead.
Lower R arm in front of torso. |

 Hatchett hint: Keep hips square and weight centered.

Part B: Demi-plié, straighten.

| 1-4 | Demi-plié (photo c). | Lift R arm side.
Turn R palm up. |
| 5-8 | Straighten legs. | |

 Hatchett hint: Keep hips square. Don't let knees roll in. Keep heels on floor and chest lifted.

a

b

c

Part C: Flat back, roll down.

1-4	Rotate torso to flat back. Rotate L leg to parallel (photo d).	Reach R arm back.
5-8	Round torso down to R leg.	Touch floor with hands.

 Hatchett hint: As the R arm reaches back, the L arm is by the ear. R arm is held at shoulder level. Lengthen neck; don't drop head. Don't let L leg rotate in past parallel. Keep weight over balls of feet.

d

Part D: Stretch R, demi-plié L, straighten.

1-8	Stretch torso toward R leg.	Hold top of R foot with L hand. Hold back of R foot with R hand.
1-8	Bend L knee (photo e).	
1-8	Straighten L leg and continue stretching.	

Hatchett hint: Relax head. Use arms for added resistance to pull torso toward leg.

Part E: Flat back, rotate front.

1-4	Lift torso to flat back stretched to front R corner.	Reach L arm overhead. Reach R arm back.
5-8	Rotate torso front. Rotate L leg out. Turn palms in.	Reach L arm overhead. Reach R arm overhead.

Hatchett hint: For the flat back, arms are held at shoulder level. Don't drop R side when rotating the torso front. Turn palms in.

e

Part F: Lift center, lower arms.

1-4	Lift torso center.	Open arms side.
5-8		Lower arms down.

Repeat entire exercise on L side.

Warm-Up #11 Runner's Stretch

Skill level:	All
Stretching:	Hip flexor (iliopsoas); underside of thigh (hamstrings); back (erector spinae group); inner thigh (adductors); calf (gastrocnemius); just below calf (soleus); top of foot (metatarsals)
Strengthening:	Top of thigh (quadriceps); back (erector spinae group)
Starting position:	Stand in forward lunge position; bend R knee; slide L leg back turned out; relax arms by sides.

Count	Movement	Arms

Part A: Release down, roll up.

1-4	Release torso down (photo a).	Round arms back. Lift elbows.
5-8	Roll torso up. R knee remains bent.	Relax arms.

Repeat part A.

◇ *Hatchett hint: Lead torso down with chest. Don't move R knee. When rolling torso, R knee remains bent.*

Part B: Release down, slide L leg back.

1-4	Release torso down.	Round arms back. Lift elbows.
5-8	Slide L leg back turned out.	Touch floor.
1-8	Hold lunge position.	

◇ *Hatchett hint: While sliding L leg, stay turned out. R knee is perpendicular to ankle.*

Part C: Rotate parallel.

1-8	Rotate L leg to parallel, R heel on floor. Stretch L hip down toward floor (photo b).	

◇ *Hatchett hint: L leg is straight. Flatten back and lengthen neck.*

Part D: Straighten, flex foot, bend knee.

1-8	Straighten R leg. Relax head down. Stretch torso toward R leg (photo c).	Straighten arms.
1-8	Flex R foot and continue stretching.	
1-8	Return to lunge position with R foot on floor, and bend R knee. Slide L leg back on ball of foot. Stretch L hip toward floor.	Bend arms.

Repeat part D 3 times.

◇ *Hatchett hint: Hands always touch floor, even if R leg does not straighten. Don't let L leg turn out. In the lunge position, keep R heel on floor and watch R knee alignment.*

Beginners and advanced beginners stop and repeat entire exercise on L side. Intermediate and advanced levels continue.

Part E: Top of foot on floor.

1-8	With top of L foot on floor, stretch L hip down toward floor (photo d).
1-8	Continue stretching.

 Hatchett hint: Stay lifted and don't let L knee touch floor. Keep R heel on floor.

Part F: Rotate back and front.

1-8	Rotate L hip and torso back. Turn out R leg slightly. Keep R heel on floor. Remain lifted on L side (photo e).	Reach R arm side.
1-8	Lift and rotate L hip and torso front. Keep R heel on floor. Turn out R leg. Stretch torso to flat back (photo f).	Lift arms side.
1-8	Continue stretching.	

 Hatchett hint: When reaching side, energy continues through fingertips of R hand. R leg turns out naturally, but don't overdo it. When rotating front, center weight and lengthen neck; don't drop head. Don't let R knee roll in.

d

e

f

37

Part G: Rotate side, arabesque, tilt front.

1-8	Rotate legs and torso R to lunge position. Bend R knee in parallel position. Slide L leg back in parallel on ball of foot.	Touch floor.
1-8	Lift L leg to arabesque. Bend R knee slightly. Lift torso to flat back (photo g).	Reach R arm front and L arm back.
1-4	Rotate hips and torso front. Tilt torso R; focus R. Lift L leg and straighten R leg.	Reach R arm to lower R corner. Reach L arm to upper L corner (photo h).
5-8	Hold tilt position.	

Hatchett hint: For the arabesque, both arms are at shoulder level. Turn palms down. When reaching arms, press shoulders down.

Part H: Passé L, relevé, hold.

1-4	Passé L leg Lift torso center.	Round arms overhead.
5-8	Relevé R leg	Open arms side. Turn palms down.
1-8	Hold relevé.	

Repeat entire exercise on L side.

Hatchett hint: Lift L knee as it bends into passé. Press shoulders down and don't drop arms as you relevé.

g

h

Skill level: Intermediate/Advanced
Stretching: Underside of thigh (hamstrings); top of foot; calf (gastrocnemius)
Strengthening: Top of thigh (quadriceps); hip flexor (iliopsoas); back (erector spinae group); stomach (rectus abdominus); inner thigh (adductors); arms (when used as resistance)
Starting position: Sit on floor; reach legs front; point feet; reach arms side.

Count	Movement	Arms

Part A: Contract, release.

Count	Movement	Arms
1-4	Contract torso back; flex feet.	Move arms front (photo a).
5-8	Release torso front, slightly past neutral; point feet.	Move arms back past sides (photo b).

Repeat part A.

 Hatchett hint: Lead arms front with heels of hands. Keep chest lifted. Release torso front slightly past neutral. Pull arms back from wrists.

a

b

 Beginners stop. Intermediate and advanced levels continue.

Part B: Pike, straighten R-L.

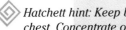

(pike position)

1-8	Bend knees to chest; point feet off floor.	Wrap arms behind knees.
1-4	Straighten R leg.	
5-8	Straighten L leg.	

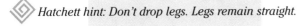*Hatchett hint: Keep back tall and press shoulders down. Use arms for added resistance to pull knees toward chest. Concentrate on controlling balance. When you straighten your legs, don't drop them. Back remains straight.*

Part C: Reach R-L.

1-4	Lift rounded R arm overhead.
5-8	Lift rounded L arm overhead.

Hatchett hint: Don't drop legs. Legs remain straight.

Part D: Circle feet out and in.

1-4	Circle feet out.
5-8	Circle feet in.

Part E: Changement, lower down, hold.

(changement)

1	Cross R leg front and L leg back.	
2-16	Changement 1 count each 15 times. Lower torso and legs toward floor.	Lower arms to shoulder level.
1-8	Hold position (photo c).	

Hatchett hint: Torso and legs lower together slowly toward the floor. When holding the position, the torso and legs are as close to the floor as possible. Keep chin off chest.

C

40

Warm-Up #13   Reach n' Press

Skill level:	All
Stretching:	Underside of thigh (hamstrings); top of foot; calf (gastrocnemius)
Strengthening:	Back (erector spinae group)
Starting position:	Sit on floor; reach legs front; point feet; relax arms by sides.

Count	Movement	Arms
Part A: Reach n' press.		
1-8	Press torso to flat back 8 times (photo a).	Reach arms front.

Hatchett hint: *Don't lift chin. Maintain flat back position. Hold arms at shoulder level and turn palms in.*

Count	Movement	Arms
Part B: Lift center, open side, contract, lift center, reach up.		
1-2	Lift torso center.	Lift rounded arms overhead.
3-4	Open rounded arms side.	
5-6	Contract torso back and flex feet (photo b).	Move arms front.
7	Lift torso center; point feet.	Move rounded arms side
8		Lift rounded arms overhead.
Repeat entire exercise.		

Hatchett hint: *Press shoulders down. Contract torso and lead arms front with heels of hands. Keep chest lifted.*

a

b

Warm-Up #14   Hamstring Stretch

Skill level:	All
Stretching:	Underside of thigh (hamstrings); inner thigh (adductors); calf (gastrocnemius); top of foot
Strengthening:	Arms (when used as resistance)—upper arm (biceps); lower arm
Starting position:	Lay on back; bend R knee to chest; reach L leg front; point feet; hold just below knee with hands.

Count	Movement	Arms

Part A: Pull R knee in, straighten.

| 1-4 | Pull R knee to chest (photo a). | |
| 5-8 | Straighten R leg (photos b1, b2). | Hold bottom of R foot and under thigh. |

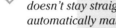 *Hatchett hint: Use arms for added resistance to pull R leg toward torso. Use all counts. Don't rush. If R leg doesn't stay straight while you hold bottom of foot, hold at calf or thigh. Don't hold behind knee. This grasp will automatically make knee bend.*

Part B: Stretch, flex foot.

| 1-8 | Stretch R leg. | |
| 1-8 | Flex R foot. Continue stretching. | |

Repeat part B 2 times.

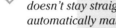 *Hatchett hint: Keep lower back and buttocks on floor. R knee should be in line with R shoulder. L leg remains straight in line with hip. Keep energy flowing through foot.*

a

b1

b2

42

Part C is an advanced stretch. Beginners and advanced beginners should skip part C and continue with part D. Do not exceed your own limitations when stretching. Pull your leg only as far as it will go naturally. The level of ability is not important; it's the level of flexibility that matters.

Part C: Flex plié, point extend.

1-4	Bend R knee to chest. Flex foot (photos c1, c2).	Hold behind R foot and knee.
5-8	Straighten R leg from knee to toe; point foot.	

Repeat part C 3 times.

 Hatchett hint: Use forearm for added resistance to keep thigh stationary while straightening R leg.

Part D: Rotate R leg out, flex foot, lower.

1-8	Rotate R leg out and stretch side (photos d1, d2).	Hold bottom of R foot.
1-8	Flex R foot and continue stretching.	

Repeat part D.

 Hatchett hint: If leg won't stay straight while holding the bottom of foot, then hold at calf or thigh. Be careful not to drop R leg side by hip, causing L hip to pop up.

1-8	Lower R leg down to floor.

Repeat entire exercise on L side.

c1

c2

d1

d2

Warm-Up #15   Changements

Skill level:	Intermediate/Advanced
Stretching:	Top of foot (metatarsals); inner thigh (adductors)
Strengthening:	Inner thigh (adductors)
Starting position:	Lay on back; reach legs to ceiling; point feet; reach arms side on floor; turn palms down.

Count	Movement	Arms

Part A: Changement, switch legs.

(changement)

1 Cross R leg front and L leg back (photo a).

2 Cross L leg front and R leg back.

Repeat part A.

◇ *Hatchett hint: Squeeze inner thighs together. Keep legs at 90-degree angle from floor. Keep lower back on floor during exercise.*

Part B: Open legs, close.

5-6 Open legs to straddle position; flex feet (photo b).

7-8 Close legs; point feet.

Repeat parts A and B 7 times.

◇ *Hatchett hint: Control legs when opening. Squeeze inner thigh muscles to resist legs closing fast. Use all counts. Don't rush.*

Part C: Open legs, stretch, flex feet.

1-4 Open legs to straddle position; flex feet (photo c). Hold inside of legs.

5-16 Stretch legs; point feet.

1-8 Flex feet and continue stretching.

◇ *Hatchett hint: Hold inside of legs so lower back remains on floor. If you have trouble holding calf, then hold inner thigh. Do not hold behind knees. This hold will automatically cause knees to bend.*

a

b

c

44

Skill level:	All
Stretching:	Front shoulder (anterior deltoid); side of torso (obliques); inner thigh (adductors); underside of thigh (hamstrings); back (erector spinae group); calf (gastrocnemius); tops of feet (metatarsals)
Strengthening:	Back (erector spinae group)
Starting position:	Sit on floor; open legs to straddle position; point feet; bend arms slightly front.

Count	Movement	Arms

Part A: Bounce shoulders.

1-16	Bounce shoulders 16 times.	

 Hatchett hint: Arms remain bent to bounce shoulders well.

Part B: Release down, roll up.

1-8	Release torso down to R leg.	Smooth R hand down top of R leg.
1-8	Roll torso up.	

Repeat part B on L side.

 Hatchett hint: Use all counts. Don't rush. Roll up from bottom of spine.

Part C: Rib cage R-L.

1-2	Move rib cage R (photo a).	Lift arms side.
3-4	Move rib cage L.	

Repeat part C 3 times.
Reduce part C using 1 count for each move. Repeat 6 times.

 Hatchett hint: Keep opposite hip on floor when moving rib cage.

a

45

Part D: Rib cage center, flat back, lift center.

1-2	Move rib cage center.	
3-8	Lean torso forward to flat back (photo b).	Lift arms slightly back.
1-8	Lift torso center.	Move arms side.

◇ *Hatchett hint: Remain in flat back and move as close to floor as possible. Lengthen neck; don't drop head. Keep knees facing ceiling. Avoid rolling knees in. Close legs slightly if knees roll in.*

Part E: Press shoulder R-L.

1	Press R shoulder front; move L shoulder back (photo c).	Hands are on floor.
2	Press L shoulder front; move R shoulder back.	

Repeat part E 3 times.

◇ *Hatchett hint: In count 1, don't force shoulder back. Concentrate on pressing shoulder front.*

Part F: Round front, drop elbows, reach up, open side.

1-2		Lift rounded arms in front of chest.
3-4		Bend arms. Drop elbows. Turn palms toward face.
5-6		Reach arms overhead. Turn palms front.
7-8		Open arms side. Turn palms down.

◇ *Hatchett hint: In counts 3-4, don't drop elbows past chest.*

b

c

46

Part G: Stretch R, rotate front.

1-8	Stretch torso over R leg (photo d).	Hold bottom or top of R foot and leg.
1-8	Rotate torso front; flex R foot (photo e).	Hold ball of R foot. Reach L arm overhead.

Repeat part G on L side.
Reduce part G on both sides, using 4 counts for each stretch.
Reduce part G on both sides 2 times, using 2 counts per stretch.
Reduce part G on both sides 4 times, using 1 count per stretch.

 Hatchett hint: When stretching over R leg, focus down to R knee, not front. L hip remains on floor. Keep knees facing ceiling. Don't let L leg roll in. When rotating front, rotate torso out by count 1 and accent L arm. L hip remains on floor. Don't drop R side. Reach L arm to upper R corner. Lengthen neck; don't drop head. Focus center.

Part H: Stretch front, roll up.

1-8	Stretch torso toward floor; point feet.	Walk hands front 8 times.
1-16	Continue stretching. Relax head down.	Reach front with hands on floor.
1-8	Roll torso up, flex feet.	Walk hands in 8 times.

Repeat part H with flexed feet.

 Hatchett hint: Relax head. Don't hold tension in the neck.

d

e

Part I: Lift groin, push forward, lower.

1-4	Lift groin off floor; flex feet (photo f).	Touch floor with R hand in front of groin, L hand behind buttocks.
5-8	Push legs and groin forward.	
1-8	Lower groin to floor; point feet.	

Repeat part I. Change hands.

f

Warm-Up #17   Battements

Skill level:	All
Stretching:	Underside of thigh (hamstrings); calf (gastrocnemius); top of foot (metatarsals)
Strengthening:	Top of thigh (quadriceps); hip flexor (iliopsoas)
Starting position:	Lay on your back; bend R knee in parallel position with heel on floor; reach L leg front on floor; point L foot; reach arms side on floor; face palms down.

Count	Movement	Arms

Battement L, lower.

1	Lift L leg (see photo).
2	Lower L leg.

Repeat entire exercise 7 times. Change legs on last battement.
Repeat entire exercise on R side 8 times.
Repeat entire exercise with flexed foot 8 times on both sides.

◇ *Hatchett hint: Keep lower back and buttocks on floor. Lift L leg up from under thigh not top of thigh. R heel remains on floor. Don't push off R foot to lift L. Relax head on floor without tension. When you lower your leg, don't let L heel smash floor. Visualize leg lifting over a barrel as it lowers to help you control the leg down.*

Skill level: Intermediate/Advanced

Stretching: Inner thigh (adductors); underside of thigh (hamstrings); back (erector spinae group)

Strengthening: Stomach (abdominals); top of thigh (quadriceps); hip flexor (iliopsoas); back (erector spinae group); arms (when used as resistance)

Starting position: Lay down on L side; reach L leg down on floor; reach R leg turned out on top of L leg; point feet; reach L arm overhead on floor, palm turned down; bend R arm in front of stomach; relax head down on L arm.

> **Beginners and advanced beginners should not attempt this exercise. Intermediate dancers should attempt only with caution. Do not exceed your own limitations when stretching and avoid pulling your leg further than it will go naturally. The level of ability is unimportant; it's the level of flexibility that matters.**

Count	Movement	Arms

Part A: Battement R, lower.

1	Lift R leg up (photo a).	
2	Lower R leg.	

Repeat part A 7 times.

 Hatchett hint: Keep R leg turned out and L leg straight throughout exercise. Lift R leg up from under thigh not top of thigh. Stay on L side and don't lean pelvis forward or backward. Keep hips even and stacked one on top of the other. When lowering your leg, don't let R foot smash on L. Visualize leg lifting over a barrel as it lowers to help you control leg down.

Part B: Battement R and flex foot, lower down.

1	Lift R leg up; flex foot.	
2	Lower R leg.	

Repeat part B 3 times.

Part C: Coupé R, passé, straighten.

1-2	Coupé R leg (photo b).	
3-4	Lift R leg to passé (photo c).	
5-8	Straighten R leg.	

 Hatchett hint: Use all counts for 5-8. Don't rush.

a

b

c

49

Part D: Stretch R leg, flex foot.

1-8	Stretch R leg (photos d1, d2). Hold heel of R foot.
1-8	Flex R foot and continue stretching.

Repeat part D.

◈ *Hatchett hint: Use arms for added resistance to pull leg closer to torso.*

Part E: Roll R on back, stretch R, flex foot.

1-8	Roll R on back; point foot (photos e1, e2).	Hold bottom of R foot and side of leg.
1-8	Stretch R leg.	
1-8	Flex R foot and continue stretching.	

◈ *Hatchett hint: Rotate R leg to chest. Don't hold behind knee. This grip will automatically make your knee bend. Keep L leg straight in front of hip.*

d1

d2

e1

e2

50

Part F: Split R, arch back, stretch over.

1-8	Roll over to R split. Stretch torso over R leg. Point feet (photos f1, f2).	Touch floor.
1-8	Lift torso center; arch back (photos g1, g2).	Reach rounded arms overhead.
1-8	Lift torso center; stretch torso over R leg.	Hold bottom of R foot.

Hatchett hint: If you have trouble with a full split, do a half split by bending L knee.

f1

f2

g1

g2

51

Part G: Roll L on back, stretch R, flex foot, lower down.

1-8	Roll L on back. Stretch R leg side (photos h1, h2).
1-8	Continue stretching.
1-8	Flex R foot and continue stretching.
1-8	Lower R leg.

Repeat entire exercise on L side.

Hatchett hint: If your leg won't stay straight while you hold the bottom of your foot, then hold outside of leg with your R hand at calf or L hand under thigh. Be careful not to drop R leg side by hip, causing the L hip to pop up. Stretching into R side will keep both hips on floor and increase range of motion. Keep L leg straight in front of hip.

h1

h2

Shoulder to Shoulder: Isolation Exercises to Warm Up Specific Body Parts and Improve Coordination

Center Exercises

#	Warm-up	Skill level	Page number
19	Head Isolations	All	54
20	Shoulder Isolations	All	55
21	Rib Cage Isolations	All	56
22	Pelvis Isolations	All	58
23	Hip Isolations	All	59
24	Focus Isolations	Beginner	60
25	Traveling Isolations	Int/Advanced	61

Skill level: All
Starting position: Stand in second position parallel with straight legs; round arms by sides.

Count	Movement	Arms

Part A: Lower head down and back.

1-4   Lower head down (photo a).   Round arms.

5-8   Lift head back.

Repeat part A.
Reduce part A using 2 counts for each direction. Repeat 2 times.
Reduce part A using 1 count for each direction. Repeat 4 times.

 *Hatchett hint: Isolate head only.*

a

Part B: Tilt R-L.

1-4   Tilt head R (photo b).

5-8   Tilt head L.

Repeat part B.
Reduce part B using 2 counts for each tilt. Repeat 2 times.
Reduce part B using 1 count for each tilt. Repeat 4 times.

Hatchett hint: Press shoulders down. When tilting head R, don't lift L shoulder; keep shoulders even. When tilting head L, don't lift R shoulder.

Part C: Look R-L.

1-4   Turn head R (photo c).

5-8   Turn head L.

Repeat part C.
Reduce part C using 2 counts for each direction. Repeat 2 times.
Reduce part C using 1 count for each direction. Repeat 4 times.

Hatchett hint: Snap head R on count 1. Hold counts 2-4.

Part D: Circle R-L.

1-16   Circle head R 2 times.

1-16   Circle head L 2 times.

b

Hatchett hint: Complete two head circles in each direction. Lengthen neck when circling back.

c

Warm-Up #20   Shoulder Isolations

Skill level: All
Starting position: Stand in second position parallel with straight legs; relax arms by sides.

Count	Movement	Arms

Part A: Lift shoulders, lower down.

1	Lift shoulders (photo a).	Lift arms away from torso.
2	Press shoulders down.	Lower arms.

Repeat part A 3 times.

 Hatchett hint: Accent shoulder lift and squeeze underarms to lift arms away from torso.

Part B: Lift R, lower down.

1-8	Lift R shoulder 4 times.	Lift R arm away from torso.
1-8	Lift L shoulder 4 times.	Switch arms.

Reduce part B using 4 counts each. Lift each shoulder twice.
Reduce part B using 1 count each 2 times. Lift each shoulder once.

 Hatchett hint: When lifting the R shoulder, don't move L arm or shoulder.

Part C: Lift R-L.

1	Lift R shoulder; press L shoulder down.	Lift R arm away from torso. Press L arm down.
&	Lift L shoulder; press. R shoulder down	Switch arms.

Repeat part C 3 times.

 Hatchett hint: Keep rib cage neutral.

Part D: Roll back and front.

1-8	Roll shoulders back 4 times.	Relax arms by sides.
1-8	Roll shoulders front 4 times.	

Part E: Roll back R-L, roll front R-L.

1	Roll R shoulder back.	Lift R elbow away from torso.
2	Roll L shoulder back.	Switch arms.
3	Roll R shoulder front.	Lift R elbow away from torso.
4	Roll L shoulder front.	Switch arms.

Repeat part E 3 times.

a

55

Part F: Bounce shoulders.

1-8	Bounce shoulders 8 times.	Bend arms slightly front.

 Hatchett hint: Arms are positioned as if playing the piano.

Part G: Rotate R in, center.

1-8	Bounce shoulders 8 times. Rotate L leg in and lift heel. Bend knees (photo b).
1-8	Bounce shoulders 8 times. Rotate L leg back front. Bend knees.

Repeat part G on L side.
Repeat part G on both sides.

 Hatchett hint: Rotate L leg in from hip.

b

Warm-Up #21   Rib Cage Isolations

Skill level: All
Starting position: Stand in second position parallel; bend knees; round arms by sides.

Count	Movement	Arms

Part A: Rib cage R-L.

1-2	Move rib cage R (photo a).
3-4	Move rib cage L.

Repeat part A 3 times.
Reduce part A using 1 count for each isolation. Repeat 4 times.

 Hatchett hint: Bend knees, center weight, and keep hips square throughout exercise to allow rib cage greater range of motion.

a

Part B: Grande plié, straighten.

1-8	Move rib cage R-L 8 times. Bend knees to grande plié turned out (photo b).
1-8	Move rib cage R-L 8 times. Straighten legs.

Hatchett hint: For the grand plié, keep heels on floor and use all counts.

b

Part C: Release, contract.

1-2	Release rib cage front. Rotate legs to parallel and bend knees (photo c).
3-4	Contract rib cage back.

Repeat part C 3 times.
Reduce part C using 1 count for each isolation. Repeat 4 times.

Hatchett hint: Accent count 3, and hold count 4.

Part D: Release, rib cage R, contract, rib cage L.

1-2	Release rib cage front.
3-4	Move rib cage R.
5-6	Contract rib cage back.
7-8	Move rib cage L.

Repeat part D.
Repeat part D moving L 2 times.
Reduce part D using 1 count each on both sides 2 times.
Accent each rib cage.

Hatchett hint: Keep hips square and weight centered.

c

Part E: Circle R-L.

1-8	Circle rib cage R 2 times.
1-8	Circle rib cage L 2 times.

Hatchett hint: Complete two rib cage circles, and keep it smooth.

Part F: Front R corner, back L corner.

1-2	Move rib cage to front R corner.
3-4	Move rib cage to back L corner.

Repeat part F.
Reduce part F using 1 count each 4 times.
Repeat part F on L side 2 times.
Reduce part F using 1 count each on L side 2 times.

Warm-Up #22   Pelvis Isolations

Skill level: All
Starting position: Stand in second position parallel; bend knees; relax arms by sides.

Count	Movement	Arms

Part A: Pulse pelvis back.

1-8	Pulse pelvis back 8 times.	

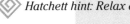 *Hatchett hint: Relax arms and maintain knee bend. Keep rib cage neutral.*

Part B: Rotate R leg in, center.

1-4	Pulse pelvis back 8 times. Rotate R leg in and lift heel. Bend knees (see photo).	Round arms back slightly.
5-8	Pulse pelvis back 8 times. Rotate R leg back front. Bend knees.	

Repeat part B on R side.
Repeat part B on both sides.

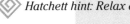 *Hatchett hint: Maintain knee bend.*

Skill level: All
Starting position: Stand in second position parallel; bend knees; reach arms down to corners; spread fingers (jazz hands); face palms front.

Count	Movement	Arms

Part A: Pulse hip R

1-8   Pulse hip R 8 times.
Bend knees (photo a).

1-8   Pulse hip L 8 times.
Bend knees.

Reduce part A using 4 counts for each side.
Reduce part A using 2 counts for each side. Repeat 2 times.
Reduce part A using 1 count for each side. Repeat 8 times.

 Hatchett hint: Accent each hip pulse. Hold last hip pulse R to start hip pulse L. Don't let shoulders or rib cage move.

a

Part B: Triple hips R.

1   Push hip R.   Lift R arm to lower corner
Bend knees.   Bend L arm with elbow side.

&   Push hip L.   Swing to switch arms.
Bend knees.

2   Push hip R; lift L heel.   Swing to switch arms.
Straighten R leg (photo b).

Repeat part B on L side.
Repeat part B on both sides.

 Hatchett hint: Accent hip push R for count 2.

Part C: Triple hips and passé R.

1   Push hip R.   Lift R arm to lower corner.
Bend L arm with elbow side.
Turn palms back.

&   Push hip L.   Swing to switch arms.

2   Push hip R; bend L knee to   Swing to switch arms.
passé (photo c).

Repeat part C on L side.
Repeat part C on both sides.

b

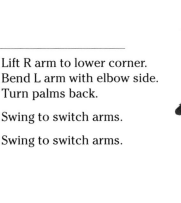

c

Skill level: Beginner
Starting position: Place R foot back and lift heel; straighten L leg; relax arms by sides.

Count	Movement	Arms

Part A: Cross R, cross L front, step R, dig L.

(traveling side)

1	Step R foot side and look R (photo a).	Round arms back; lift elbows.
2	Cross L foot over R and look L (photo b).	
3	Step R foot side and look R.	
4	Dig L foot next to R and look center.	

Repeat part A moving L.
Repeat part A on both sides 2 times.

Hatchett hint: When focusing R, keep shoulders and hips square. Accent the head movement. Make leg motions fluid, not isolated and choppy.

a

Part B: Three-step turn R.

(turning R)

1	Step R foot side; look R.	Lift arms side.
2	Cross L foot side; turn to face back.	Round arms front.
3	Step R foot side; turn to face front.	Open arms side.
4	Dig L foot next to R and look center.	Clap hands 1 time in front of chest.

Repeat part B on L side.
Repeat part B on both sides.

Hatchett hint: Spot (look) R throughout turn (counts 1–3).

b

Skill level: Intermediate/Advanced
Starting position: Place R foot back and lift heel; relax arms by sides.

Count	Movement	Arms

Part A: Dig step R, look R, look center.

(traveling front)

1	Dig R foot next to L.	Relax arms with relaxed fist.
&	Step L foot front.	
2	Dig R foot next to L; look R (photo a).	
&	Step L foot front; look center.	

 Hatchett hint: In count 1, keep R knee bent with weight over balls of feet. This is a traveling movement. Travel on the step but not on the dig. Work on executing feet first, then add head and torso isolations.

a

Part B: Dig step R, lift shoulders L-R.

3	Dig R foot next to L.	
&	Step L foot front.	
4	Dig R foot next to L (photo b).	Lift L shoulder and press R shoulder down. Bend arms front.
&	Step L foot front.	Switch shoulders.

 Hatchett hint: Accent the shoulder isolations.

Part C: Dig step R, slap thighs R-L, snap fingers 2 times.

5	Dig R foot.	Lower R shoulder.
&	Step L foot front.	
6	Dig R foot next to L.	Slap R thigh.
&	Step L foot front.	Slap L thigh.
7	Dig R foot next to L.	Snap fingers with both hands once.
&	Step L Foot front.	
8	Dig R foot.	Snap fingers with both hands once.
&	Step L foot front.	

b

 Hatchett hint: Shoulders square. Relax as you slap thighs. Snap fingers in front of chest.

Part D: Walk front and look R to L, down to center; 90s camel walk R-L; step front R-L.

1	Step R foot front and look R.	Relax arms.
2	Step L foot front and look L.	
&	Look center.	
3	Step R foot front and look down.	
4	Step L front and look center.	

◈ *Hatchett hint: Make head isolations clean and precise.*

(90s camel walk 2 times)

5	Step R foot front with straight leg; press hip out. Bend L knee and lift heel. Lean torso slightly forward (photo c).	Lift L shoulder; press R shoulder down. Bend arms front.
6	Step L front with straight leg. Bend R knee and lift heel.	Switch shoulders.
7	Step R foot front. Release torso front.	Roll shoulders back.
8	Step L foot next to R. Move torso center.	Press shoulders down.

◈ *Hatchett hint: Don't lean torso too far forward. Lean just enough to feel the energy go out R hip.*

c

d

Part E: Walk back and move rib cage R-L-contract-release.

1	Step R foot back and lift heel. Move rib cage R (photo d).	Touch thighs with fingers. Lift elbows side.
2	Step L foot back and lift heel. Rib cage moves L.	
3	Step R foot back and lift heel (photo e). Release torso front.	
4	Step L foot back and lift heel (photo f). Contract torso back.	

 Hatchett hint: Make the four walks smooth.

Part F: Push hips R-L, pas de bourrée R.

5	Step R foot back and lift heel. Push hip R.	
6	Step L foot back and lift heel. Push hip L.	

(pas de bourrée)

7	Cross R foot behind L.	Place hands on hips with thumbs forward.
&	Step L foot side on ball of foot.	
8	Step R foot side.	

 Hatchett hint: On the & count, keep weight centered not over L leg.

e

f

CHAPTER 4

Basic Movements

Not only does Frank fine tune your instrument, but his in-your-face energy gives you the tools you need to take any audition by storm and walk away with a job! *−Cornell Ivey, teacher and choreographer*

Now that your body is warmed up, put on your jazz shoes. But before you put the music on, take a few moments to read how to best use this chapter.

Each movement exercise includes the starting position, counts, movement, arms, and Hatchett hints (technique pointers). The starting position is very important to learning the movement properly. Starting the movement incorrectly will make it harder to learn. You also risk falling behind the music. You want to feel great from the time you start to move, so begin with the starting position. The counts, movement, and arms come next. The counts are provided to help you learn the timing of the movement. The movement column is where you learn how your body moves. Part of the movement is learning how the feet should work. Learning the foot work before incorporating the arms makes movements easier to pick up and helps to develop coordination. Once you involve the arms, the feet should begin to work naturally and, eventually, automatically. Getting the foot work first is especially important when learning

more challenging and rhythmic movements. It also makes it easier to concentrate on torso, arm, and head movements and the artistic interpretation they contribute.

Next, we offer Hatchett hints. These hints will help you focus on proper alignment and technique, address the most common areas for improvement, and provide tips or secrets to make the movements come alive. Dancers and choreographers understand that frequently just a subtle hint makes all the difference in understanding how to stylize the movement.

The movements in this chapter are not just for the beginner dancer. The movements presented here are valuable for everyone, regardless of your technical ability, especially if this style of jazz dance is not familiar to you. Just as with any other dance form, the basics are very important. Once you have learned these basic movements, it will be easier to pick up the beginner, advanced beginner, and intermediate/advanced movements in the chapters ahead.

Let's get started!

Starting position

Place R foot back and lift heel; relax arms by sides.

Count	Movement	Arms
	(traveling forward)	
1	Cross R foot over L and lift heels.	Relax fists. Punch L arm front. Bend R arm back (see photo).
2	Cross L foot over R and lift heels.	Relax fists. Punch R arm front. Bend L arm back.
	Repeat entire movement.	

Hatchett hints

Continue to lift the heels (i.e., relevé) as you walk forward. Use your strength to punch the arms forward. Keep the legs straight without locking the knees.

#2   Attitude Walk

The Attitude Walk is a smooth movement that makes a statement. It's based on a display of feeling. So feel confident and act sassy. Let that powerful attitude show on your face.

Starting position

Place R foot back and lift heel; relax arms by sides.

Count	Movement	Arms
	(traveling forward)	
1	Step R foot front and lift heels.	Lift R arm side leading with elbow. Lower L arm (see photo).
2	Step L foot front and lift heels.	Lift L arm side leading with elbow. Lower R arm.
	Repeat entire movement.	

Hatchett hints

Keep the knees bent as you walk. Visualize walking in 5-inch heels to keep the heels lifted.

#3 Butterfly

The Butterfly is a basic street movement. This move is smooth, so keep your transitions (moving from one count to another) fluid. Feel the move coming from your soul (your spirit) to get into the groove.

Starting position

Stand with feet hips-width apart; relax arms by sides.

Count	Movement	Arms
&	Rotate knees and feet in.	Bend arms. Lift shoulders and elbows side.
1	Push pelvis forward. Follow with hip and torso as knees start rotating out.	Cross arms in front of chest (photo a). Lift arms to open (photo b).
2	End with knees rotated out. Lower heels slightly (photo c).	End with arms side.

Repeat entire movement.

 Hatchett hints

A slight lift occurs in the body and arms on the "&" count when rotating the knees in. Let the shoulders move with the arms. It's difficult to rotate in with straight legs, so be sure to keep the knees bent throughout. Lift the heels to help rotate the knees from the hips.

Variations

- Place both hands on the knees and do the Butterfly.
- Place the R hand on the floor and the L hand on the hip. Rotate just the R knee in and out. Repeat on the other side.

a

b

c

#4　Cabbage Patch

The Cabbage Patch is a basic street movement. This move is great for loosening up the rib cage and learning to shift your weight fluidly.

Starting position

Place R foot back and lift heel; relax arms by sides.

Count	Movement	Arms
&	Step R foot side and lift heel. Move rib cage L. Shift weight L.	Circle arms R in front of chest (photo a).
1	Circle rib cage R. Shift weight R.	Pull arms in (photo b).
2	End with rib cage L. Shift weight L.	End with arms R (photo c).

Repeat on L side.

◈ Hatchett hints

The pulling action of the arms makes the rib cage circle. The arms start circling, then the rib cage follows. Visualize the arms churning butter, with the torso as the mixer.

a　　　　b　　　　c

70

The Contemporary Wrap requires attitude.

Starting position

Stand in second position parallel; relax arms by sides.

Arms

Wrap R arm over L holding side of L shoulder (see photo).

 Hatchett hint

Keep the elbows lifted.

Variations

- Wrap 1: Wrap the R arm overhead with the palm facing down and the elbow side; relax the L arm by your side. Don't cover the face with the R arm.

- Wrap 2: Wrap the R arm overhead with the palm facing down and the elbow side; wrap the L arm under the chest with the palm facing in.

- Body Wrap: Wrap the R arm under the chest with the palm facing in; wrap the L arm back with the palm facing out.

The Cosmic Slop is a basic street movement. When first learning the movement, say to yourself, "jump it out, jump it in." Vocalizing this phrasing will help you understand the rhythm and timing of the movement.

Starting position

Stand in first position parallel; bend knees; relax arms by sides.

Count	Movements	Arms
1	Jump side to lunge R. Rotate torso to R corner. Weight is centered (photo a).	Lift arms side with fists.
2	Jump into first position parallel. Rotate torso center (photo b).	Cross arms in front of chest.

Repeat on L side.

 Hatchett hints

Be light on the feet to avoid getting stuck in the lunge position. Keep the arms away from the torso when lifting side.

Variation

Instead of crossing the arms in front of the chest, lower them by your sides. Keep the arms bent throughout.

a

b

Starting position

Stand in second position parallel; relax arms by sides.

Movement	Arms
Rotate R leg in from pelvis and lift heel. Straighten L leg; weight is centered.	Cut R arm side from shoulder with fingers spread (jazz hand). Place L hand on hip (see photo).

◈ Hatchett hints

Don't lock the L leg. The Cut is strong, with energy shooting out through the fingers. The jazz stance will enhance the strength and power of the Cut. Cutting with the downstage arm (arm closest to the audience) adds more style and flavor.

Variations

The arms can either be straight or bent depending on how much power is needed.

Cut on count 1, then add a head snap front on count 2 to give the Cut move more attitude and power.

Starting position

Stand with feet together; relax arms by sides.

Count	Movement	Arms
1	Dig R foot back and lift heel. Swivel hips R (photo a).	Circle arms overhead R.
2	End facing R side in second position parallel (photo b).	End with arms down.

Repeat on same side.

◇ *Hatchett hints*

The swivel is a smooth movement. Let it flow. Swivel the hips and then let the torso follow.

a

b

Starting position

Stand in second position parallel; relax arms by sides.

Movement	Arms
Rotate R leg in and lift heel. Rotate torso L; weight is centered.	Flick R hand away from torso. Place L hand on hip (see photo).

 Hatchett hints

Visualize flicking water from your fingertips. The action comes from the wrist. The hand starts relaxed, then becomes strong at the end of the Flick. The Flick adds flavor and spice to your dancing.

Variations

- You can flick the hands in any arm position.
- Flick both hands overhead 2 times to the R with the palms facing down. Twist the legs L 2 times, keeping the weight on balls of the feet.

Starting position

Place L foot back and lift heel; relax arms by sides.

Count	Movement	Arms
&	Hop L foot side.	Circle L hand in.
1	Bring R foot next to L. Move pelvis back (photo a).	Circle R hand in. Circle L hand out.
2	Lower R heel; bend knees (photo b).	Alternate circling hands in L-R.

Repeat on same side.

◇ Hatchett hints

Circle the arms close to the torso.

To really "Get Jiggy," you must let go and feel it from within. Infuse the move with spirit. This movement should be loaded with flavor and attitude.

a

b

Starting position

Stand in second position parallel; relax arms by sides.

Arms

Reach hands side, palms facing front, with fingers spread (see photo).

 ### Hatchett hints

Don't fan fingers back. Send energy through the fingertips. Keep the arms at shoulder level, not below, to give the position more strength and power. Stylize a movement by incorporating the Jazz Hand.

Variations

- Arms can be held in any position.
- Lift Jazz Hands in front of face with elbows bent to the side. Place the R hand above the L with the palms facing out. Look out through the fingertips.

Starting position

Stand in second position parallel; relax arms by sides.

Movement	Arms
Rotate R leg in from pelvis and lift heel. Bend knees; weight is centered.	Round arms back. Lift elbows (see photo).

Hatchett hints

Initiate the lift and rotation of the R leg from the pelvis and hip not the knee. Starting the move correctly places the body in proper alignment and will naturally lift the R heel. Don't let the L leg turn out or you will lose stability. Keep both knees bent to promote strength and ensure smooth transitions to other movements.

Variation

You can add a variety of arms. Put on some music and play with different arm positions.

Starting position

Stand in second position parallel; relax arms by sides.

Movement	Arms
Rotate R leg in and lift heel. Rotate torso L. Lean weight toward R leg.	Press heel of hand to front R corner with a straight arm. Bend L arm and place hand near hip (see photo).

◇ Hatchett hints

Send the energy through the heel of the hand by flexing the wrist. Push the R arm up from the shoulder. The Jazz Wrist Press can be used in all levels.

Variation

Press the heels of both hands side. The Jazz Wrist Press can be used in any position.

79

Starting position

Place R foot back and lift heel; relax arms by sides.

Count	Movement	Arms
&	Jump on R foot. Contract torso back slightly.	
1	Touch L foot next to R. Release torso front (see photo).	Bend R arm. Reach L arm to upper L corner.
&	Jump on L foot. Contract torso back slightly.	
2	Touch R foot next to L. Release torso front.	Bend L arm. Reach R arm to upper R corner.
&	Jump on R foot. Contract torso back slightly.	
3	Touch L foot next to R. Release torso front.	Bend R arm. Reach L arm to upper corner.
&	Contract torso back.	
4	Release torso front.	

Repeat on L side.

◇ Hatchett hints

Add a bounce by keeping the knees bent with the weight over the balls of the feet. This generates more energy and flavor. Squeeze the inner thighs together as you touch.

Variation

Instead of doubling up on the third Jump Touch (R-L-R-pulse R), make them all single jump touches (R-L-R-L) or single, double, single (R-L-pulse L-R).

Starting position

Stand in first position parallel; relax arms by sides.

Count	Movement	Arms
1	Cross R foot behind L. Place weight on ball of R foot.	Bend arms into chest (photo a).
&	Step L foot side; lift R foot. Shift weight onto ball of L foot.	Open arms side (photo b).
2	Step R foot side. Shift weight R (photo c).	
Repeat on L side.		

◈ Hatchett hints

Don't shift your full weight onto the L foot. Keep the weight on the balls of the feet. When first learning the pas de bourrée, keep the arms lifted side.

a   b   c

Raise the Roof originated from the movement "Push it Up."

Starting position

Place R foot back and lift heel; relax arms by sides.

Count	Movement	Arms
1	Step R foot side. Bend knees. Focus R (photo a).	Push arms up. Flex hands back at wrists.
2	Touch L foot next to R. Straighten knees slightly (photo b).	Push arms up.

Repeat on L side.
Repeat on R and L sides.

◈ Hatchett hints

Relax, feel the music, and release your inhibitions. Get funky! Add a bounce by keeping the weight over the balls of the feet. This generates move energy and flavor.

Variation

Start in second position parallel. With hands flexed back at wrists, push up the arms R 2 times and lean the torso R (counts 1-2). Push up the arms L 2 times and lean the torso L (counts 3-4). Repeat the arms. Push up the arms high, but keep them slightly bent. Keep the weight centered and the knees bent.

a

b

Starting position

Place R foot back and lift heel; relax arms by sides.

Count	Movement	Arms
(reach–pull)		
1	Bend knees; step R foot side. Move rib cage R (photo a).	Reach R arm front and move to side.
2	Shift weight L. Pull rib cage L.	Grab air with hand and pull R arm into side.
(cha, cha, cha)		
3	Dig R foot in (photo b).	Place hands on hips.
&	Dig L foot next to R.	
4	Dig R foot in place.	
Repeat on the L side.		

Hatchet hints

The Cha, Cha, Cha part of the movement has a Spanish flair.

When first learning, say, "reach, pull, cha, cha, cha." Vocalizing the steps will help you to understand the correct rhythm and timing.

Don't stop the momentum when you pull into the Cha, Cha, Cha. Let the movements flow together without losing control. Don't let the arms reach side above shoulder level.

Variations

You will find other variations of the Cha, Cha, Cha in the advanced beginner and intermediate/advanced level movements described in chapters 6 and 7.

a

b

Starting position

Place R leg back and lift heel; relax arms by sides.

Count	Movement	Arms
1	Lunge R. Move rib cage R (see photo).	Reach R arm up to R corner. Reach L arm down.
2	Lunge L. Move rib cage L.	Reach L arm up to L corner. Reach R arm down.

Repeat entire movement.

Hatchett hints

When first learning this movement, concentrate on getting the arms and legs and then add the rib cage. Keep the arms strong when reaching to the corners. Don't let the wrists drop. Continue sending energy through the fingertips. Hold the legs in a lunge position to give the rib cage more freedom to move.

Variation

You can double up the Rib Reach. Reach R-L-R-pulse R (counts 1, 2, 3, 4).

The Run, Run, Run is a basic street movement that was influenced by the pas de bourrée.

Starting position

Stand in second position parallel; relax arms by sides.

Count	Movement	Arms
(running pas de bourrée)		
1	Cross R foot behind L; lift L knee. Face front R corner (photo a).	Bend arms front. Bounce shoulders 1 time.
&	Step L foot side; lift R knee. Face front (photo b).	Bounce shoulders 1 time.
2	Step R foot side. Face front R corner (photo c).	Bounce shoulders 1 time.
Repeat on L side.		

◇ Hatchett hints

In class, Frank will say, "Pas de boo hoo, run, run, run," to help them relax and have fun with this movement.

Execute the Run, Run, Run as if you're running. Keep the knees bent with the weight over the balls of the feet. Lift the knees but not to hip level. Keep the arms loose and relaxed to bounce the shoulders more freely.

a

b

c

This movement is also known as the Tootsie Roll, which is a basic street movement.

Starting position

Place R foot back and lift heel; relax arms by sides.

Count	Movement	Arms
1	Step R foot side . Rotate L knee in and lift heel (see photo).	Bend arms front. Bounce shoulders twice.
2	Step L foot side. Rotate R knee in and lift heel.	Bounce shoulders twice.

Repeat entire movement.

◈ Hatchett hints

The Shoulder Bounces require feeling and spirit. Let it go and feel the music, without losing control. Bend the arms and relax to bounce the shoulders more freely.

Variations

- With feet apart, step R-L-R with 6 shoulder bounces. Jump the feet together as you clap the hands 1 time (counts: 1, 2, 3, jump and clap 4).

- A variety of leg movements can be incorporated with the shoulder bounces: Step R foot side, bring R foot in next to L, step L foot side, bring L foot in next to R. Bounce shoulders 8 times.

- A jazz square or step touch can be incorporated with the Shoulder Bounces. Create your own movements.

Starting position

Place R foot back and lift heel; relax arms by sides.

Count	Movement	Arms
1&	With a deep knee bend, step R foot side. Lean torso R (photo a).	Slap thighs twice.
2	Step R foot together next to L.	Wrap arms across chest. Hold sides of shoulders (photo b).

Repeat on L side.

◈ Hatchett hints

The Slap Wrap is a great basic movement to learn attitude and improve strength. Get low on the slap, and do it with attitude. Accent the wrap and keep the elbows lifted.

a

b

#22 Slice

Starting position

Face L front corner. Place R foot back and lift heel; relax arms by sides.

Count	Movement	Arms
1	Touch R foot front. Bend L knee (photo a).	Swing L arm up to front L corner. Swing R arm back.
2	Touch R foot back. Bend L knee (photo b).	Swing R arm up to corner. Swing L arm back.
	Repeat entire movement.	

 Hatchett hints

Keep weight on the supporting leg and bend the knee throughout. Always touch with the leg closest to the mirror or the audience. Relax. Add a bounce by keeping knees bent and weight over balls of the feet. This adds more energy and flavor. Visualize the arms slicing through the air, always swinging in opposition. Remember, the L arm is front when the R foot is front and the R arm is front when the R foot is back.

Variation

Instead of holding the arms straight, bend and swing them front and back. This will give the Slice a funkier flavor. Add the bounce.

a   b

Starting position

Place R foot back and lift heel; relax arms by sides.

Count	Movement	Arms
1	Step R foot front and lift L heel. (photo a).	Reach arms overhead to V position
2	Pivot half turn L facing back (photo b). Place weight on L foot and lift R heel.	Swing arms down; cross in front of chest.
3	Set R foot front facing back and lift L heel.	Reach arms overhead to V position.
4	Pivot half turn L facing front. Place weight on L foot and lift R heel.	Swing arms down; cross in front of chest.

Repeat on R side.

◈ Hatchett hints

When you pivot, never lift the balls of the feet off the floor. The heels, however, do lift as you pivot. Keep the knees bent throughout. Accent the V position arms. Keep the shoulders down and the hips square to the front. Be sure not to lead with the hip or shoulder.

Variation

Pivot around the room with a quarter turn to face each wall. Step the R foot front as the arms lift side. Pivot L to face the side wall as the arms swing down and cross in front of the chest and the head swings L. Step the R foot front to face the side as the arms lift side. Pivot L to face the back wall as the arms swing down and cross in front of the chest and the head swings L. Repeat the step pivot to the back wall, then side, then front.

a

b

The basic Step Touch is a wonderful movement for first learning to loosen up and feel the music.

Starting position

Place R foot back and lift heel; relax arms by sides.

Count	Movement	Arms
1	Step R foot side (photo a).	Reach arms overhead to V position.
2	Touch L foot next to R (photo b).	Lower arms by sides, palms facing front.

Repeat on L side.

 Hatchett hints

Never put your full weight on a touch; instead, place the weight only on the balls of the touching foot. Visualize the touching foot landing in either very hot or very cold water so that you must move it away to begin the Step Touch to the other side.

Add a bounce by keeping the knees bent and the weight on the balls of the feet. This generates more energy and flavor.

Place the arms in a V position. Don't fling them out of control. Keep the shoulders down.

Variations

You can add any arm movement:

- Reach the arms side as you step the foot side.
- Cross the arms in front of the chest as you cross and touch the foot back, or cross the arms down in front of the pelvis as you cross and touch the foot back.
- Cross the arms in front of the chest as you step the foot side.
- Pull the arms in to the waist with fists as you touch in.
- Use Whack, Whack arms (see chapter 6, page 129) as you step touch.

a

b

Starting position

Stand in second position parallel; relax arms by sides.

Movement	Arms
Rotate L knee out and lift heel. Focus (look) R (see photo).	Lift R arm side. Bend L arm in front of chest.

◈ Hatchett hints

The Strike is used to enhance an accent in the music.

The legs, arms, and head are executed at the same time with strength and attitude. The weight is centered, not placed over the L leg. Concentrate on lifting the L heel.

Variations

- The Strike can be done on demi-pointe (see photo) or on pointe (tip of toe). You can add a variety of arm positions.
- Change the legs but use similar arms. Strike a Jazz Stance (see page 78). Bend L arm in front of chest. Reach R arm up to R corner with heel of hand. Focus over L shoulder.

Starting position

Place R foot back and lift heel; bend both arms front and relax hands.

Count	Movement	Arms
	(twist legs)	(alternating shoulder lifts)
1	Step R foot side. Rotate legs R and lift heels. Move rib cage R.	Lift R shoulder (see photo). Press L shoulder down.
	(traveling forward)	
&	Step L foot front. Rotate legs L and lift heels. Move rib cage L.	Lift L shoulder. Press R shoulder down.
2	Step R foot front. Rotate legs R and lift heels. Move rib cage R.	Lift R shoulder. Press L shoulder down.
	Repeat on L side.	

Hatchett hints

Keep the weight on the balls of the feet with knees bent and heels lifted. Accent the third shoulder lift (count 2). Bend the arms and relax to move the shoulders. Freedom of movement in the shoulders will help the rib cage to move naturally and freely.

Starting position

Place R foot back and lift heel; relax arms by sides.

Count	Movement	Arms
1	Step R foot side. Rotate L leg in and lift heel. Snap head R (see photo).	Throw arms down R.
2	Shift weight L. Rotate R leg in and lift heel. Snap head L.	Throw arms down L.

Repeat entire movement.

Hatchett hints

The Throw, Throw is not a wild movement. Keep the arms loose and relaxed without losing control and making them look wild.

Accent the head snap to give the movement flavor and style. Don't let the head drop straight down; instead, look out and down.

Starting position

Stand in second position turned out; relax arms by sides.

Movement	Arms
Lift heels in relevé (see photo).	Reach arms overhead with palms facing out.

Hatchett hints

V-position arms create a very strong line. Continue the energy through the fingertips. Don't break the hands at the wrist. Keep the shoulders down and space between the ears and arms.

Variation

Any foot position can be done with V-position arms. Palms can also face inward.

Starting position

Stand in second position parallel; relax arms by sides.

Count	Movement	Arms
1	Push hips R (see photo).	Bend and whip arms R from the elbows.
2	Push hips L.	Whip arms L from the elbows.
Repeat entire movement.		

Hatchett hints

Keep the knees bent to give the hips more freedom to move. Whip the arms from the elbows. Don't just move the arms and legs; move the rib cage, shoulders, and head as well. Let it go and feel the music.

Sample Phrases

Below are two examples of how phrases or basic choreography are created by stringing together various movements. We choreographed four sets of eight counts for each example. Concentrate on making smooth transitions and letting the movements flow together. All the movements presented here were covered in this chapter.

Example #1

Count	Movement
12345678	Afro Crosswalks 8 times R, L, R, L, R, L, R, L
&12&34&56&78	Butterfly 4 times
12345678	Step Touch 4 times R, L, R, L
1 hold 2	Contemporary Wrap
3 hold 4	Jazz Hand
5 hold 6	Cut
7 hold 8	Flick

Example #2

Count	Movement
&12&34&56&78	Cabbage Patch 4 times
123&4567&8	Reach Pull Cha, Cha, Cha 2 times R, L
12	Dig Swivel (end facing R side)
345678	Rib Reach 6 times facing R side R, L, R, L, R, L
12345678	Raise the Roof 4 times and end facing front R, L, R, L

CHAPTER 5

Beginner Movements

If you can do the Hatchett style, then you can do any type of dance. Frank uses ballet, jazz, and ethnic dance and combines it all to create his own style. —Mamie Duncan Gibbs, Broadway's Chicago

Congratulations! You've made it through the basics and are now ready for beginner moves. This chapter introduces more directional changes and syncopated movements. Remember to relax, let it go, and get down, but stay in control. Have fun and VOP!

Explore It: Improving Beginner VOP-Style Moves

Starting position

Place R foot back and lift heel; relax arms by sides.

Count	Movement	Arms
1	Step R foot side. Release and contract torso (photo a).	Place hands on thighs with fingers spread.
2	Step R foot together next to L. Release and contract torso (photo b).	
3	Step L foot side. Release and contract torso.	
4	Step L foot together next to R. Release and contract torso.	

Repeat entire movement.

 Hatchett hints

Don't let the elbows drop into the sides of the torso. Touch the thighs lightly with the hands.

Variation

The feet remain the same. Step the R foot side as you make a half circle with the R arm (from side to front) and pull the hand into the waist with a fist. Bring the R foot next to the L as you reach the R arm overhead and pull into the waist with a fist. Step the L foot side as you reach both arms overhead and pull into the waist with a fist. Bring the L foot next to the R as you make a half circle with the L arm (from side to front) and pull into the waist with a fist.

a

b

99

Starting position

Place R foot back and lift heel; relax arms by sides.

Count	Movement	Arms
1	Step R foot to front R corner and lift heel. Lift L leg to parallel passé (photo a).	Pull L arm into side with palm facing up. Reach R arm front.
(ballchange)		
&2	Step L foot back and lift heel. Step R foot front (photo b).	Reach L arm front. Lower R arm back.

Repeat on same side.

◈ Hatchett hints

The Bow and Arrow is a traveling movement. The line of movement looks best when you are traveling on an angle, not directly front.

a   b

Starting position

Place R foot back and lift heel; relax arms by sides.

Count	Movement	Arms
1	Step R foot front and lift heels. Center the weight.	Lift L arm front. Lift R arm back. Spread fingers (jazz hands) (photo a).
&	Step L foot in place.	
2	Step R foot back and lift heel.	Lift L arm back. Lift R arm front. Spread fingers (jazz hands) (photo b).
&	Step R foot in place.	

Repeat on same side.

◇ Hatchett hints

Keeping knees bent and heels lifted throughout will help you feel the rhythm. Spread the fingers without tension so the arms don't become rigid.

a

b

Starting position

Stand in second position parallel; bend knees; relax arms by sides.

Count	Movement	Arms
1	Move rib cage R. Straighten legs slightly. Center the weight (photo a).	Bend R arm up to corner; flick hand. Place L hand on thigh.
&	Move rib cage L. Bend knees (photo b).	Bend R arm into chest. Twist wrist L.
2	Move rib cage R. Bend knees deeper (photo c).	Bend R arm down to corner; flick hand.
&	Move rib cage L. Straighten legs slightly.	Bend R arm into chest. Twist wrist L.

Repeat on same side.

◇ Hatchett hints

Visualize reaching your arm up to get cookies from the shelf and then reaching down in the refrigerator to get the milk. If teaching this movement to adults, call it "Pretzels and Beer" instead.

When first learning say, "Up and down" (counts 1&2&), "cookies n' milk." You don't always need to rely on counts. Saying words to the rhythm of the counts gets you in the groove. Feel the spirit from within and get down!

Flick the hand from the wrist.

a

b

c

Starting position

Assume jazz stance. Rotate R leg in from pelvis and lift R heel; bend knees; weight is centered; relax arms by sides.

Count	Movement	Arms
1	Push hips to front R corner. Focus R; weight is centered (photo a).	Circle in and swing R arm up to R corner. Snap fingers 1 time.
&	Push hips L.	Circle in and swing R arm down.
2	Push hips to front R corner (photo b).	Finish swinging R arm down to R corner. Snap fingers 1 time.
&	Push hips L.	Circle and swing R arm L up.

Repeat on same side.

Hatchett hints

This is a great first movement to learn to help loosen up the torso, shoulders, and hips.

Hip pulses stem from the isolation portion of the warm-ups (see page 53, chapter 3).

To stylize this move, you have to feel it from within and give it attitude.

Pulse your hips to the corner not side. Accent the finger snaps and hip pulses R. Don't lower the R heel when snapping down. Keep the torso facing the L front corner; don't rotate the torso to face front. Make sure the R arm cirles L half way down and R half way up. Relax the torso and feel the groove.

Variation

Start with the feet in second position parallel. Bend and turn out the R knee with the heel lifted. Place the hands on the hips. Start by lifting the hips up R ("&" count). Pulse the hips L 8 times (counts 1-8). Accent the hip pulse L. Lift the arms overhead through second position as you pulse the hips 8 times. Lower the arms through second position as you pulse the hips 8 times. Allow the rib cage and shoulders to move naturally.

a

b

Starting position

Stand in second position parallel; relax arms by sides.

Count	Movement	Arms
1-2	Twist heels R 2 times. Pulse hips R 2 times. Lean torso slightly forward (see photo).	Clasp hands. Pulse R elbow side 2 times.
1-2	Twist heels L 2 times. Pulse hips L 2 times. Lean torso slightly forward.	Pulse L elbow side 2 times.

Repeat entire movement.

 ### Hatchett hints

Feel the music and let it go.

Place the weight on the balls of the feet. Keep the torso forward throughout so that the rib cage is easier to move. Let the rib cage move naturally.

Starting position

Place R foot back and lift heel; relax arm by sides.

Count	Movement	Arms
1	Hop out to wide second position parallel. Lean torso forward, weight over balls of feet (photo a).	Round arms back. Lift elbows.
&	Hop into first position parallel (photo b).	
2	Hop out to wide second position parallel.	

Repeat entire movement.

◈ Hatchett hints

From the VOP standpoint, don't hop up and down; instead, hop into the floor. Keep the movement on the same level, so make sure you hop into a wide second position.

The arms are important to support the style. Keep them placed, not moving up and down. When first learning (if needed), place the hands on the hips to get a feel for the rhythm. Then add the arms. Keep the knees bent and the weight over the balls of the feet.

a

b

105

#8   Penguin

Starting position

Place R foot back and lift heel; relax arms by sides.

Count	Movement	Arms
	(ball change in second throughout)	
&1	Step feet apart R-L; bend knees. Circle rib cage R (see photo).	Alternate shoulders rolling front R-L. Place hands on thighs.
	Repeat entire movement.	

◈ *Hatchett hints*

The Penguin stems from the rib isolation portion of the warm-ups (see page 56, chapter 3).

Learn the feet first (ball change), then add the rib cage and shoulder rolls. Keep the weight over the balls of the feet throughout. Accent the rib cage movement on count 1. Don't allow the elbows to drop into the sides of the torso.

#9   Reach Wrap

Starting position

Place R foot back and lift heel; relax arms by sides.

Count	Movement	Arms
&1	Step R foot side; step L foot side. Lift heels (photo a).	Reach arms overhead to corners.
2	Rotate R leg in and lift heel. Bend knees; weight is centered. Focus (look) down (photo b).	Wrap R arm front. Wrap L arm back with palm facing out.
3	Rotate R leg out to second position. Lift heels (photo c).	Reach arms side with fingers spread.
4	Rotate L leg in and lift heel. Bend knees; weight is centered (photo d).	Clasp hands R with straight arms.

Repeat entire movement.

◈ Hatchett hints

Make sure you step to a wide second position. Make the arms strong on the reach up (count &1), reach side (count 3), and clasped hands (count 4). Keep the weight centered, especially on the wrap and clasp.

a

b

c

d

This movement was originally created by M.C. Hammer and called "the Hammer."

Starting position

Stand in first position parallel; relax arms by sides.

Count	Movement	Arms
&	Lift and bend R leg to passé. Lift L heel with straight leg (photo a).	Lift and bend elbows side with relaxed fists.
1	Lower R leg and slide L leg back Lift heel. Lean torso slightly forward (photo b).	Push arms down with relaxed fists.
	Repeat on L side.	

◇ Hatchett hints

Doing the Running Man helps bring out your spirit. Make sure to attach the R foot to the side of the L leg. Slide the L leg back at the same time the R foot makes contact with the floor, not before. Both feet remain in parallel throughout. The arms help generate energy by being strong on the lift. Keep the space between the forearms and torso small.

a

b

#11 Sky to Earth

This movement was one of the very first movements that Frank ever taught.

Starting position

Place R foot back and lift heel; relax arms by sides.

Count	Movement	Arms
(pony R-L-R)		
1	Step R foot side. Rotate torso R (photo a).	Push arms up to sky.
&	Step L foot next to R.	Bend arms in halfway.
2	Step R foot side.	Push arms up to sky.
(pony L-R-L)		
3	Step L foot side (photo b). Rotate torso L and lean down.	Push arms down to earth.
&	Step R foot next to L.	Bend in arms halfway
4	Step L foot side.	Push arms down to earth.
Repeat entire movement.		

◇ Hatchett hints

Add a bounce by keeping the knees bent and the weight over the balls of the feet. This generates more energy, flavor, and spirit.

Variation

Counts 1&2 (pony R-L-R) remain the same. On counts 3&4, cross the L foot over the R, step R side, cross the L over the R as you push the arms down 2 times L.

a   b

Starting position

Stand in second position parallel; relax arms by sides.

Count	Movement	Arms
(ripple)		
&	Tilt head R.	Bend arms side.
1	Lift head center. Lift rib cage. Lift L hip and heel (photo a).	Lift L arm naturally back. Roll L shoulder back.
2	Move shoulder and rib cage center. Lift L heel (photo b).	
	Repeat on L side.	

◈ Hatchett hints

The Snake is fluid and smooth. Make sure head tilts and then lifts center to start the ripple.

a

b

Starting position

Place R foot back and lift heel; relax arms by sides.

Count	Movement	Arms
1	Step R foot side (photo a).	Reach arms overhead to V position.
&	Cross L foot over R.	
2	Step R foot side (photo b). Bend knees and lift L heel. Snap head R.	Throw arms down.

Repeat on L side.

◈ Hatchett hints

Bend the arms into the shoulders to throw them down. Don't throw the arms directly side. Relax the arms to make the throw; try not to stiffen up. Accent the throw and head snap.

Be sure to emphasize the difference in levels (high and low). The reach up is high (counts 1&), and the throw is low (count 2).

Variation

For counts 1 and 2, step, together, step: Step R the foot side as you reach the arms overhead. Step the L foot next to the R. Step the R foot side as you throw the arms down R and snap the head R.

a

b

111

Starting position

Place R foot back and lift heel; relax arms by sides.

Count	Movement	Arms
		Bend arms front.
1	Step R foot side (photo a).	Lift L shoulder; press R shoulder down.
&	Step L foot near R (photo b).	Lift R shoulder; press L shoulder down.
2	Step R foot side (photo c).	Lift L shoulder; press R shoulder down.

Repeat starting left.

◈ Hatchett hints

Keep the arms bent to allow the shoulders to move easily. Accent the third shoulder lift. Let the movement go and feel the music.

Variations

- You can add the Triple Shoulders to many movements. The Triple Shoulders remain the same, but the feet change. Start in second position parallel and center your weight. Do Triple Shoulders R-L-R (counts 1&2). On count 2 turn out and bend the R leg. Lift the R heel, and look over the R shoulder. As you repeat the Triple Shoulder to the L, rotate the R leg back to parallel. Turn out the L leg on count 2.

- Step the R foot side as you alternate shoulder lifts 2 times (R-L) (count 1). Touch the L foot next to the R as you alternate shoulder lifts 2 times (R-L) (count 2). Repeat on the L side.

a

b

c

Starting position

Place R foot back and lift heel; relax arms by sides.

Count	Movement	Arms
&	Step R heel side.	Reach R hand in a fist to L corner at chest level.
1	Step L heel side (photo a). Lean torso slightly forward.	Swing R arm through chest level to R side. Reach L arm side with a fist.
2	Rotate L leg in and lift heel. Bend knees. Contract torso R (photo b).	Wrap L arm front. Wrap R arm back with palm facing out.

Repeat on L side.

◈ Hatchett hints

The arms resemble a windmill motion going through chest level. Lean the torso slightly forward to maintain balance and control. Accent the arms in second position (count 1). Don't anticipate the rotation of the torso and L leg until count 2. Accent the arms again in the wrap position.

Variation

Do the windmill arms overhead without fists. Turn the feet out in second position with the heels lifted as the arms circle overhead R. End with a drag (L leg drags in next to R) as the arms lower down by your sides.

a

b

Starting position

Stand in second position parallel; relax arms by sides.

Count	Movement	Arms
1	Circle R knee out 2 times. Circle hips R 2 times (photo a).	Circle R arm R 2 times. Place L hand on thigh.
2	Lower R heel down as you finish circles (photo b).	Finish R arm out to side.
(pas de bourrée)		
3	Cross R foot behind L.	Swing R arm down in front of torso. Swing L arm down in back of torso.
&	Step L foot side.	
4	Cross R foot front.	Swing L arm down in front of torso. Swing R arm down in back of torso.
Repeat on L side.		

◈ Hatchett hints

Relax and feel the music to help you get into the groove. Visualize washing a window in a circular motion. Don't let the R arm drop below waist level. The shoulder lifts naturally.

Variation

Stand with feet apart and knees bent. Alternate circling in with both hands. Circle the R hand in ("&" count). Circle the L hand in as the R hand circles out (count 1). Lift the shoulders as you circle the hands in and lower the shoulders as you circle the hands out. Feel the rhythm and let the torso groove.

a

b

114

Sample Phrases

Here are two examples of how phrases or basic choreography are created by stringing together various movements. We choreographed four sets of eight counts for each phrase. Concentrate on making smooth transitions and letting the movements flow together. All the movements in these phrases were covered in this chapter.

Example #1

Count	Movement
1&23&45&67&8	Triple Shoulders 4 times R, L, R, L
&12&34	VOP Windmill 2 times R, L
&5&6&7&8	Running Man 4 times to front L corner R, L, R, L
1&23&45&67&8	Sky to Earth 4 times to face front R, L, R, L
12345678	Afro Side Step 4 times R, L, R, L

Example #2

Count	Movement
1&2&3&4&	Choo Choo 2 times R to front L corner
5&67&8	Bow and Arrow 2 times R to front L corner
1&2&3&4&	Choo Choo 2 times R
5&67&8	Bow and Arrow 2 times R
&12&34&56&78	Snake 4 times to face front R, L, R, L
&1234	Reach Wrap R
5&6&7&8	Hip Pulses 4 times R

CHAPTER 6

Advanced Beginner Movements

Frank Hatchett is the angel who gave me my wings of passion to the entertainment industry. Without him I would have never found the key that opened my life.   *—Gretchen Palmer, actress, Diet Pepsi "Uh-huh" girl*

Up to now we've concentrated on learning how the legs, arms, and body work together. Now that you have learned the basics, it's time to learn more challenging moves. Concentrate on stylizing the movements by fusing attitude and projection while connecting with the music.

Starting position

Place R foot back and lift heel; relax arms by sides.

Count	Movement	Arms
1	Step R foot front. Focus L (photo a).	Clap hands 2 times
2	Step L foot front.	Clap hands 1 time.
3	Hop out to second position parallel. Focus center (photo b).	Place fists on hips.
&	Hop into first position parallel.	
4	Hop out to second position parallel.	

Repeat entire movement.

Hatchett hints

The Flamenco Attitude is an example of character attitude with a Spanish flair. It's a basic walk, but moving with attitude gives the walk flavor and feeling. Keep the chest and head lifted to display attitude and confidence.

When first learning, clap out the rhythm. Accent the third clap.

Don't hop up and down on the out-in-out; instead, keep the knees bent and the weight over the balls of the feet, and hop to a wide second position. This will help keep the body from moving up and down.

The Flamenco Attitude is a great movement for improving coordination and working across the floor with progressions.

a

b

#2 Giddy Up

The Giddy Up is simply a fun movement. Learning this movement helps you to become light on your feet.

Starting position

Place R foot back and lift heel; relax arms by sides.

Count	Movement	Arms
	(ball change in second position throughout)	(lasso arms)
&1&2	Step feet apart R-L 2 times. Bend knees (photo a).	Circle R arm overhead L 2 times. Place L hand on hip.
&3	Ball change (photo b).	Whip R arm front.
&4	Ball change.	Whip R arm side.
&5	Ball change.	Whip R arm back.
&6	Ball change.	Whip R arm side.
		(lasso arms)
&7&8	Ball change 2 times (photo c).	Circle arms overhead R 2 times.

◈ Hatchett hints

Feel the music and let yourself go. Keep the knees bent with the weight over the balls of the feet throughout.

a   b   c

Starting position

Place R foot back and lift heel; relax arms by sides.

Count	Movement	Arms
(face front and travel side)		
&	Lift R foot front (photo a).	Roll L shoulder front. Move R shoulder back.
1	Step on R foot.	
&	Lift L foot front.	Roll R shoulder front. Move L shoulder back.
2	Cross L foot over R.	
&	Lift R foot front.	Roll L shoulder front. Move R shoulder back.
3	Step on R foot.	
(ball change)		
&4	Cross L foot behind R and lift heel. Step on R foot. Lean torso forward (photo b).	
Repeat traveling L.		

◇ Hatchett hints

The Hatchett Walk is a smooth movement. This movement starts on the downbeat (the "&" count), which gives the walk its flavor, rhythm, and style. Lift the foot off the floor; don't make it a kick. Travel with small steps only.

a

b

Starting position

Place R foot back and lift heel; relax arms by sides.

Count	Movement	Arms
1	Dig R heel to front R corner. Bend L knee. Lean torso back (photo a).	Reach L arm to corner with fingers spread (jazz hand). Place R hand on hip.
&	Hop on R foot.	
2	Touch L foot next to R. Round torso over (photo b).	Bend R arm front. Move L arm back.

Repeat on L side.

Hatchett hints

Make the heel dig small enough to keep the weight over the L leg. Make sure the torso starts with a lean back and ends by rounding forward. Never put any weight down on the touch.

Variation

The feet remain the same except the heel dig is front. Dig the R heel front as you cross the hands front at chest level with fists. Hop on the R foot as you begin pulling the arms into the hips. Touch the L foot next to the R, and finish pulling the arms into the hips.

a

b

Starting position

Stand in parallel position with the feet hip-width apart; relax arms by sides.

Count	Movement	Arms
&	Twist legs R. Flex R foot; lift L heel. Rotate torso R (photo a). Focus (look) R; weight is centered.	Bend R arm side. Lift L arm side.
1	Twist legs front (photo b).	Bend arms slightly back.
2	Hold.	
	Repeat on L side.	

◈ ***Hatchett hints***

Start the leg twist in the hips not the knees. Accent the "&" count.

a

b

Starting position

Place L foot back and lift heel; relax arms by sides.

Count	Movement	Arms
&	Jump off floor. Bend L knee up toward chest.	Reach arms side.
1	Kick R leg up. Lower L leg down (see photo).	
2	Step down on R foot.	

Repeat on same side.

 Hatchett hints

Hold the back straight; don't lean the chest forward to meet the knee. Kick up with a straight leg. Hold the arms strong and press the shoulders down; the arms shouldn't move up and down as you move the legs.

Variations

- You can add any arm movements to the Hitch Kick as long as they don't lower your energy or take away from kicking the leg.
- Hitch kick while staying low to the floor. Lift the R knee a little off the floor. Hitch kick the L leg as the R foot contacts the floor with the heel lifted.

Starting position

Place R foot back and lift heels; relax arms by sides.

Count	Movement	Arms
(reach pull)		
1	Step R foot side; bend knees. Move rib cage R (photo a).	Reach R arm front and move to side.
2	Shift weight L. Pull rib cage L.	Grab air with hand and pull arm into side.
(pas de bourrée)		
3	Cross R foot behind L (photo b).	Swing R arm down in front. Swing L arm down in back.
&	Step L foot side.	
4	Cross R foot in front of L.	Swing L arm down in front; Swing R arm down in back.

Repeat on the L side.

Hatchett hints

This movement builds from the basic Reach Pull Cha, Cha, Cha (page 83, chapter 4). Keep the momentum going when you pull into the pas de bourrée. Let the transitions flow without losing control. Keep the R arm at shoulder level, not above.

Variation

You will find a variation in the intermediate/advanced movements in chapter 7 (page 148).

a

b

Starting position

Place R foot back and lift heel; relax arms by sides.

Count	Movement	Arms
1	Step R foot front. Bend L knee and lift heel (photo a)	Bend arms back. Shimmy shoulders.
&	Pivot L and lift R foot slightly.	
2	Chug R foot forward (photo b). Lean torso and weight to R leg.	

Repeat pivoting L.

Hatchett hints

Keep the L knee bent and the heel lifted. This way you can lift your R leg slightly off the floor to chug forward. Relax the arms so that you can shimmy the shoulders freely.

Variations

- Place the hands on top of the thighs, and bend the arms with the elbows lifted side. Push your R shoulder front 1 time each as you pivot chug on the R foot. The L shoulder naturally moves back.

- Extend the arms straight down and slightly away from your sides. Press the R shoulder down and lift the L shoulder 1 time each as you pivot chug on the R foot.

a

b

Starting position

Stand in first position parallel; relax arms by sides.

Count	Movement	Arms
1	Hop out to wide second position parallel. Lean torso slightly forward (photo a).	Reach arms side and spread fingers (jazz hands).
&	Hop in place.	
2	Hop into first position parallel. Lean torso slightly forward (photo b).	Wrap R arm over L holding side of shoulders (Contemporary Wrap).
&	Hop out to wide second position parallel. Lean torso slightly forward.	Reach arms side and spread fingers.
3	Hop in place.	
&	Hop into first position parallel. Lean torso slightly forward.	Wrap R arm over L holding side of shoulders.
4	Hop out to wide second position parallel. Lean torso slightly forward.	Reach arms side and spread fingers.

Hatchett hints

When first learning, say, "out-out, in, out-out, in, out." Vocalizing the steps will help you understand the rhythm and timing of the movement.

If executed with straight legs, Syncopated Jacks will incorrectly look like jumping jacks and your timing will be off.

Keep the knees bent and jump to a wide second position so the movement stays on the same level; it will also be easier for you to keep the torso forward and the weight centered over the balls of the feet.

Keep the arms strong. Don't let them drop below shoulder level. Keep the elbows lifted when crossing front.

a

b

Starting position

Stand in second position parallel; relax arms by sides.

Count	Movement	Arms
1	Rotate R leg in and lift heel. Rotate torso R (photo a).	Lift bent arms side.
&	Rotate leg front. Rotate torso center (photo b). Straighten legs.	Lower arms.

Repeat on L side.

◈ Hatchett hints

Feel the groove and get down. Don't lock the legs on the "&" count.

Variation

Place the R foot back and lift heel. Relax the arms by your sides. Step the R foot front as you pull the arms up to the chest with elbows side (count 1). Step the R foot back as you lower the arms halfway (count 2). Ball change: Step the L foot back as you pull the arms up (count 3). Step the R foot in place as the arms lower halfway (count 3&). Step the L foot front as you pull the arms up (count 4).

a   *b*

Starting position

Stand in second position parallel; bend knees; relax arms by sides.

Count	Arms
&	Circle wrists in and up as elbows lift side (photo a).
1	Lift arms behind head (photo b).
&	Circle wrists in and down as elbows start coming into sides.
2	Lower arms by sides (photo c).

Repeat entire movement.

◇ Hatchett hints

When first leaning, practice just circling the wrists in-up, in-down. Once you add the arms, concentrate on keeping them relaxed, which will make it easier to Whack. Hold the hands in fists throughout; otherwise the movement will look sloppy. Accent count 1 when the fists are in the "up" position.

Variations

- You can add the Whack, Whack to many movements.
- Alternate Whack, Whack arms. Don't wait until one arm finishes whacking down before you begin whacking the other arm up.
- Step the R foot side as you whack both arms up. Touch the L foot behind the R as you whack both arms down.
- Jump to second position parallel as you whack both arms up. Jump into first position parallel as you whack both arms down.

a

b

c

Sample Phrases

Here are two examples of how phrases or basic choreography are created by stringing together various movements. We choreographed four sets of eight counts for each example. Concentrate on making smooth transitions and letting the movements flow together. All the movements presented here were covered in this chapter.

Example #1

Count	Movement
123&4567&8	Flamenco Attitude 2 times
&1&2&3&4&5&6&7&8	Giddy Up
1234	Shimmy Pivot Chug R 4 times (moving L)
567&8	Reach Pull Pas de Bourrée L (facing back)
1234	Shimmy Pivot Chug 4 times R (moving L)
567&8	Reach Pull Pas de Bourrée L (facing front)

Example #2

Count	Movement
1&2&3&4&	Under Pump 4 times R, L, R, L
&56&78	Hitch Kick 2 times L to front L corner
&1&2&3&4	Whack, Whack 2 times front
&5 hold6&7hold8	Heel Twist 2 times R, L
1&23&45&67&8	Heel Dig 4 times R, L, R, L
1&2&3&4	Syncopated Jacks
&5&6&7&8	Whack, Whack 2 times

CHAPTER 7

Intermediate and Advanced Movements

Frank always wanted the most from his dancers because he knew our capabilities. He always told us, "There is no such thing as 'I can't'."
–Sondra M. Bonitto, Broadway's Ragtime

You are now ready for intermediate and advanced movements. This chapter will challenge you with more difficult movements. Technique really counts here, so practice, practice, practice!

Remember to incorporate the spirit of the dance into your moves. Feel the music and discover your unique flavor.

Starting position

Stand in second position turned out in demi-plié; hold the arms in second position and spread fingers (jazz hand).

Count	Movement	Arms
1-3	Chug forward 3 times.	Shimmy hands.
&	Snap head R.	
4	Snap head center as you chug forward 1 time.	
5-6	Chug forward 2 times.	
7	Frog jump (see photo).	Clap hands overhead 1 time.
&	Land in second position turned-out; plié.	Open arms to V position with palms front.
8	Hop into wide second position turned out; plié.	Open arms second with fingers spread.

Repeat entire movement.

◇ Hatchett hints

Lead with the heels as you chug forward while staying in demi-plié. Keep the arms straight in second position as you shimmy the hands; the arms should not lead you forward in the chug. Accent the head snap. Keep the arms strong by pressing shoulders down in the back and sending energy through the fingertips; don't drop them below second position after the frog jump.

Starting position

Place R foot back and lift heel; relax arms by sides.

Count	Movement	Arms
1-2	Attitude the L leg back, turning R in relevé (see photo).	Circle arms overhead R.
3	Cross L foot in front of R.	Reach L arm side; round R arm front.
4	Hold.	

Hatchett hints

Stretch the arms as they circle. This keeps you lifted and gives you the momentum to turn. Be careful not to whip yourself into the turn. Don't step out of the turn until count 3 and keep the chest lifted and the energy high.

Variations

- The Attitude Turn can be done with many variations. Try a double or triple turn depending on your ability.
- Pitch (tilt) the torso R with the L leg in attitude. Reach the arms in second position.
- Add an attitude front with any arm variation.

Starting position

Place R foot back and lift heel; relax arms by sides.

Count	Movement	Arms
1	Battement R leg front in relevé. (photo a).	Reach arms overhead to V position
2	Half turn L. Passé R leg in parallel (photo b).	Bend L arm front; reach R arm side.
3	Hold.	
(ball change)		
&4	Step R foot back and lift heel. Step L foot front.	
Repeat entire movement.		

◇ Hatchett hints

Keep the energy flowing through your fingers when you battement. Stay in relevé by lifting through the supporting leg. Be sure to attach the passé foot to the side of the L leg, and accent the arms to control and hold the position.

a

b

Starting position

Place R foot back and lift heel; relax arms by sides.

Count	Movement	Arms
1	Stomp R foot front (see photo).	Move L arm front. Move R arm back.
&	Stomp L foot in place.	Lift elbows up slightly.
Da	Stomp R foot next to L.	
Repeat on L side.		

Hatchett hints

This movement has a Spanish flair. Exude confidence and attitude. Stay in plié.

Variations

- Many arm variations can be added to the Brazilian Samba.
- Visualize holding a skirt. Sway the arms side to side.
- You could also bend the arms overhead in fifth position with the elbows side and palms facing up.

Starting position

Place R foot back and lift heel; relax arms by sides.

Count	Movement	Arms
1-2	Step R foot front and lift L heel. Lean torso to R leg (see photo). Focus front.	Shimmy shoulders. Slide L arm down R leg to knee. Relax R arm down behind torso.
&	Lift torso halfway. Focus down.	Lift arms away from torso to switch.

Repeat on L side.

◇ Hatchett hints

The Cool Walk is in half time, which takes 2 counts per step. Make the walk smooth, flowing, and controlled. Don't rush. Use all the counts. Keep the focus front.

Starting position

Stand in fourth position parallel; place L foot front and lift R heel. Lift R arm front and L arm side.

Count	Movement	Arms
1-2	Outside turn with R foot in coupé.	Round arms in first position (see photo).
3&4	Pas de bourrée R-L-R.	Open arms and reach L arm front and R arm back.

Repeat on L side.

 ### Hatchett hints

Attach the R foot to the L ankle. If the foot is not attached, it will be harder for you to control the turn. Don't let the R foot move up the leg to the shin. Stay turned out in the R leg; keep pressing the knee out.

The arms and feet work together; don't execute the feet, then the arms. Lift the arms and chest as you come out of the turn to control the transition into the pas de bourrée.

Starting position

Place R foot back and lift heel; relax arms by sides.

Count	Movement	Arms
1	Touch R foot side. Lean torso forward (photo a).	Flick R hand away from torso. Place L hand on hip.
2	Hold.	
3&4	Pas de bourrée R-L-R (photo b). Lean torso slightly forward.	Push L arm front. Move R arm back.
&5&	Pas de bourrée L-R-L. Lean torso slightly forward.	Push R arm front. Move L arm back.
(ball change)		
6	Step R foot back. Lift L foot off floor. Lean torso back (photo c).	Bend arms front.
&	Step L foot front. Lift torso center.	
7	Step R foot front (photo d).	Move L arm front. Move R arm back.
8	Step L foot next to R.	Relax arms.

◈ Hatchett hints

Stay light on your feet so you can feel and add style to the movement. When first learning, say, "1, 2, pas de bourrée, pas de bourrée, ball change, step, step." Vocalizing will help you understand the rhythm and timing of the movement. It's harder to feel the accents in the rhythm when just thinking about the counts.

a

b

c

d

Starting position

Place R foot back and lift heel; relax arms by sides.

Count	Movement	Arms
1	Rotate legs in and lift heels (photo a).	Bend R arm up; bend L arm down.
&	Rotate legs out and lower heels (photo b).	Bend L arm up; bend R arm down.
2	Rotate legs in and lift heels (photo c).	Cross R arm over L.
&	Rotate legs out and lower heels. Lean torso forward (photo d).	Pull hands to hips.
3&4&	Repeat.	
5	Rotate legs in and lift heels (photo e).	Punch R arm overhead.
&	Rotate legs out and lower heels (photo f).	Punch L arm overhead. Pull R hand into side.
6	Rotate legs in and lift heels (photo g).	Flex R wrist by face. Pull L hand to hip.
&	Rotate legs out and lower heels (photo h).	Push R flexed wrist side.
7	Twist R leg out (photo i).	Swing arms overhead L. Snap fingers 1 time.
&	Twist legs L and lift heels (photo j).	Swing arms R. Snap fingers 1 time.
8	Twist R leg out and lift heel . Rotate L leg to parallel (photo k).	Swing arms down L. Snap fingers 1 time.

Hatchett hints

The Homework Coordination Step is quick, smooth, and flowing. When first learning, work on perfecting the feet before adding the arms. The barre is a great tool for learning proper alignment of the legs and feet. Face the barre, and hold on with both hands.

Rotate the legs from the hips, not the knees. The heels will lift up naturally if starting the rotation in the hips. Keep the weight lifted when rotating and lower the heels. Don't get stuck.

Starting position

Place L foot back and lift heel; relax arms by sides.

Count	Movement	Arms
1	Développé L leg and grand jeté (see photo).	Reach arms overhead to V position.
&	Land on L foot.	Start lowering arms side.
2	Cross R foot in front of L.	Lower arms completely.
Repeat on same side.		

Hatchett hints

Concentrate on these hints to stay suspended in air:

- As you concentrate on leaping out on the R leg, also focus on lengthening the L leg and keeping it in the air as long as you can.
- Send energy out both feet. Keep chest lifted.
- Place the arms. Don't let them reach back, causing you to arch the back.

Variations

- You can add many different arm variations to the Grand Jeté. Be creative.
- Grand jeté the R leg without a développé; instead lift off with a straight leg.
- Grand jetés can be done with elevation (height) or low to the floor (traveling).

Starting position

Stand in fourth position parallel; place L foot front and lift R heel. Lift R arm front and L arm side.

Count	Movement	Arms
	(parallel inside turn)	
1-2	Lift R leg to parallel passé. Turn L in relevé on L leg.	Arms are in first position.
3-4	Place R foot next to L. Bend knees.	Round arms down.
	(parallel outside turn)	
1-2	Lift R leg to parallel passé (see photo). Turn R in relevé on L leg.	Arms are in first position.
3-4	Place R foot next to L. Bend knees.	Round arms down.

Hatchett hints

Make sure to attach the arch of the R foot to the side of the L leg at the knee. This will keep the hips square.

The arms and legs work at the same time. Don't bring the arms in and then attach the R foot to turn. Avoid winding up the arms to prep for the turn. Be sure to spot.

Watch how much energy you give to a turn. Not much energy is required, especially to accomplish a triple turn. It's all about the control and the technique.

Always remember, it takes a long time to master turns. One day you're on and the next day you're off. Don't get discouraged; having good days and off days is normal.

Variation

You can add any arm movements. Be creative.

Starting position

Place R foot back and lift heel; relax arms by sides.

Count	Movement	Arms
1	Step R foot side.	
2	Step L foot next to R (photo a).	Bend arms side with fists.
3&da4	Contract torso from the pelvis 4 times (photo b).	Move arms forward naturally.
	Repeat on L side.	

◇ Hatchett hints

The Kibee Kibee is a tension movement. Squeeze the buttocks during the quick contractions. Think of fluttering the pelvis. Make sure the arms don't work too much but move only as a natural result of the contraction. You're not pounding on a door. Relax and let yourself go.

a

b

144

Starting position

Place R foot back and lift heel; relax arms by sides.

Count	Movement	Arms
1	Battement R leg front in relevé (photo a).	Reach arms overhead to V position.
2	Layout and arch back (photo b).	Sweep arms down and lift back to V position.

Hatchett hints

Make sure the back is arched. Lengthen the R leg as you lay out. Push the weight forward over the L leg. Keep the L knee bent.

a   *b*

The 90s Camel Walk stems from the original camel walk. The camel walk originated from the swing era of the 1940s as a part of social dance.

Starting position

Place R foot back and lift heel; relax arms by sides.

Count	Movement	Arms
1	Step R foot front and lift L heel. Press hips R. Lean torso slightly forward (see photo).	Lift L shoulder. Press R shoulder down.
	Repeat on L side.	

 Hatchett hints

Accent the shoulders and hips. The hip presses to the back corner, not side. The torso leans slightly forward, which helps the shoulders and hips move freely.

#14   Pump

The Pump stems from the camel walk, which originated in the swing era of the 1940s as a part of social dance.

Starting position

Place L foot back and lift heel; bend arms front.

Count	Movement	Arms
1	Hop on L leg to front L corner. Drag R foot to L ankle (see photo).	Circle shoulders and arms front.

Repeat on R side.

◈ Hatchett hints

Executing the Pump to the corner looks better from an audience viewpoint than doing the Pump straight front. Keeping the arms bent provides the momentum to travel forward. Accent pressing the shoulders down after you circle them front. Attach the R foot to the L ankle on the drag.

Starting position

Place R foot back and lift heel; relax arms by sides.

Count	Movement	Arms
1	Step R foot side; bend knees. Move rib cage R (photo a).	Reach R arm front and move to side.
2	Shift weight L. Pull rib cage L.	Grab air with hand and pull R arm into side.
3&4	Pas de bourrée turn R (R-L-R) (photo b)	Bend arms side with fists.

Repeat on L side.

Hatchett hints

Keep the momentum going into the pas de bourrée turn. Let the movements flow together without losing control and getting sloppy.

Do the pas de bourrée right underneath you.

Variation

Instead of a pas de bourrée turn, do two chaîné turns R.

a

b

Starting position

Stand in second position turned out slightly; relax arms by sides.

Count	Movement	Arms
1-2	Lunge L (photo a).	Push R shoulder toward L leg 2 times.
3-4	Lift torso (photo b). Rotate L leg out and lift heel.	Circle R arm overhead ending by side. Reach L arm overhead; focus up to L hand.

Repeat on R side.

Hatchett hints

The Rhythmic Shoulder Push uses middle and high levels. Accent the two shoulder pushes. Avoid rounding back during the shoulder push. The L shoulder moves back naturally as the R shoulder pushes front.

a   *b*

Starting position

Place R foot back and lift heel; relax arms by sides.

Count	Movement	Arms
&	Kick R foot front. Twist torso R (see photo).	Bend arms side. Move L arm toward front.
1	Step R foot in. Twist torso back to center.	Move L arm side.
&	Step L foot in place.	
2	Step R foot in place.	
&	Kick L foot front. Twist torso L.	Move R arm toward front.
3	Step L foot in.	Move R arm side.
&	Step R foot in place.	
4	Step L foot in place.	
&	Kick R foot front. Twist torso R.	Move L arm toward front.
5	Cross R foot behind L. Twist torso center.	Move R arm front. Move L arm back.
(ball change with a small hop)		
&6	Cross L foot behind R. Cross R foot in front of L.	Move L arm front. Move R arm back.
&7	Cross L foot in front of R. Cross R foot behind L.	Move R arm front. Move L arm back.
&8	Cross L foot behind R. Cross R foot in front of L.	Move L arm front. Move R arm back.
Repeat starting L.		

◇ *Hatchett hints*

The Salsa has a Spanish flair. It's quick, smooth, and loaded with flavor. Stay light on the feet, with your weight centered over the balls of the feet. Keep the legs slightly bent; the movement can't be done if the legs remain straight. The torso and arms work together. As the torso twists the arms move with it.

Starting position

Stand in second position parallel; bend knees; relax arms by sides.

Count	Movement	Arms
&	Step R foot in.	Bend R arm side. Reach L arm side.
Da	Step L foot side. Lift R foot off floor.	
1	Lunge R (see photo).	Pull R hand toward shoulder. Press L shoulder front.

Repeat on L side.

◈ Hatchett hints

The Salsa Footwork starts on the downbeat (the "&" count). When first learning, clap out the rhythm. Clapping will help you understand the rhythm and timing of the movement.

The feeling is light and the movement is quick. Take small steps and keep the weight over the balls of the feet.

Variation

Do Salsa Footwork to R-L sides 2 times (counts: &da1, &da2, &da3, &da4). Do 1 time to the front. Don't lunge. Step together R-L (counts: &da). Step front on the R foot (count: 5). Turn L and do 2 times facing the back. Don't lunge. Step L foot in place. Bring R foot next to L (counts: &da). Step L foot front (count: 6). Step R foot in place. Bring L foot next to R (counts: &da). Step R foot front (counts: 7). Turn L and do 1 time facing front. Don't lunge. Step L foot in place. Bring R foot next to L (counts: &da). Step L foot front (count 8).

151

Starting position

Place L foot back and lift heel; relax arms by sides.

Count	Movement	Arms
1	Step L foot side.	Lift arms to second position.
2	Cross R foot in front of L (photo a).	Swing arms down; cross in front of chest.
3	Développé L leg; jump to second position (photo b).	Lift arms to second position with fingers spread facing front (jazz hand).
&	Land on R foot.	
4	Cross R foot in back of L (photo c).	Lower R arm and round front.

Hatchett hints

Keep chest lifted as you jump. Keep torso up straight not forward. Don't let arms drop below shoulder level. Land with weight over R leg and lift L heel.

Variation

After count 4, full turn L to end front while keeping balls of feet in contact with the floor. L leg is front with R heel lifted.

a

b

c

Starting position

Place R foot back and lift heel; relax arms by sides.

Count	Movement	Arms
1	Step R foot side (photo a).	Reach R arm front to corner.
2	Cross L foot behind R.	Pull R arm in.
(ball change with a small hop)		(Begin to swing arms L.)
&	Cross R foot behind L.	Swing R arm down in front.
3	Cross L foot in front of R (photo b).	Reach L arm side.
&	Cross L foot behind R.	Start to swing arms R.
4	Cross R foot in front of L.	Swing L arm down in front. Reach R arm side.

Repeat on L side.

◇ Hatchett hints

Be light on the feet during the ball change. The Grapevine is quick and smooth. Move on one level; don't bobble up and down.

a

b

Starting position

Place R foot back and lift heel; relax arms by sides.

Count	Movement	Arms
1-2	Chaîné turn R in plié (photo a).	Lift arms to second and then first position.
3	Axle jump turn R (photo b).	Reach arms second. Lift R arm overhead. Bring arms to rounded first position.
&	Land on L foot.	Start opening arms side leading with heels of hands.
4	Step R foot side (photo c).	End with arms in second position. Rotate arms front with a jazz wrist press.

Repeat on L side.

 ### Hatchett hints

Use the arms to give you the momentum to turn. Keep the chest lifted and torso straight. As you jump, lift the R knee then the L. When landing, imagine opening a curtain with the heels of the hands.

Variation

Execute an axle jump without turning or a chaîné-turn preparation. Step the R foot side as you lift the arms to second position (count 1). Cross the L foot in front of the R as you swing the arms down and cross at the chest (count 2). Axle jump as you lift the arms overhead with the heels of the hands turned up (count 3). Land on the L foot as you begin to lower the arms down ("&" count). Step the R foot side as you lower the arms down by your sides (count 4).

a   b   c

Starting position

Place R foot back and lift heel; relax arms by sides.

Count	Movement	Arms
1-2	Chaîné turn R in plié.	Lift arms into second and then first position.
&	Stag leap R (see photo).	Reach arms overhead to V position.
3	Land on R foot.	Start lowering arms.
4	Cross L foot in front of R.	Reach L arm side; round R arm front.

Repeat entire movement.

◇ Hatchett hints

The arms help you to stay lifted and remain in the air longer. Reach them up to keep up the energy of the jump.

Both knees are bent when you stag. Whip the L leg around to the front before you step onto it.

Variations

- As you finish count 4, do an outside turn on the L foot, pulling the R leg into parallel passé.
- Execute the stag leap without turning or a chaîné-turn preparation. Step the R foot side as you lift the arms to second position (count 1). Cross the L foot in front of the R as you swing the arms down and cross the chest (count 2). Stag leap R as you circle the arms overhead R ("&" count). Land on the R foot as you reach the L arm side and round the R arm front (count 3). Cross the L foot in front of the R as you lower the arms down by your sides (count 4). Don't leap off the floor with both feet; lift the R and then the L.
- Any movement can be done before taking a stag leap, for example, turns, battements, step-crosses, and so on.

Sample Phrases

Here are two examples of how phrases or basic choreography are created by stringing together various movements. We choreographed four sets of eight counts for each example. Concentrate on making smooth transitions and letting the movements flow together. All the movements presented here were covered in this chapter.

Example #1

Count	Movement
123&4567&8	Afro Chug
12345678	Rhythmic shoulder push 2 times R
12	Hold
34	Pump 2 times R, L
5&da6&da7&da8	Brazilian samba 4 times R, L, R, L
&1&2&3&4&5&6&7&8	Salsa

Example #2

Count	Movement
12&34&56&78	Cool Walk 4 times R, L, R, L
123&4	Second Jump
56	Unwind L to end front
78	Inside parallel turn L
12	Walk forward to front L corner R, L
3&4	Grand Jeté R to front L corner
5678	Attitude Turn R to end front
1234	90s Camel Walk 4 times R, L, R, L to front R corner
567&8	Battement Passé R front corner to end L back corner

CHAPTER 8

Put It Together With VOP

One thing I learned from Frank is that music offers more than entertainment. When I begin to feel music, I begin to feel peace in the midst of chaos. And in this peaceful state I am able to choreograph my daily steps. *–Katherine Coleman Clark (aka DC)*

Now that you have learned the movements, you are ready to create combinations and fuse them with the spirit of the dance. Don't feel you have to perfect the movements and style before you start creating your own choreography. Perfection comes later. First, learn each movement by itself; then string the movements together into combinations. Then practice, practice, practice! Next, add style to the movements, which is what VOP is all about. Once this is accomplished, go one step further. Start creating your own movements. Begin to apply what you learned in chapter 2 from "Music Matters" (page 11), and let your creative juices flow.

Create It: Connecting Movements and Creating Combinations

The following four-step approach is suggested for learning how to get started on creating your own combinations.

1. *Acquaint yourself with the music.* Pick music that you really like and are going to feel. Keep your audience in mind—Frank always does. Now, put on the music and try a series of basic step touches. Listen and feel the music as much as possible. Relax. At first, let the arms do whatever comes naturally. Then, add the bounce. Bend the knees and keep the weight over the balls of the feet. Keep feeling the music. Create the marriage between the music and the movement. Think of your body as an instrument expressing the music through movement. Once you're comfortable with the step touch, add a step touch crossing back. Then add a step touch crossing front. Start creating and applying different arms. Feel the music. Express yourself. Make it your own.

2. *Experiment with different rhythms that capture the feeling of the music.* Listen for the mood changes and accents in the music to help you create your own dance. Allow the rhythm, melody, and mood of the music to

Movements must connect with the music, and the movement must define the music.

guide your movements. Make sure your transitions from one movement to another are smooth. A great way to help your transitions flow is to improvise with the music. This is where you create with no preplanned choreography—just dance! This will develop your self-expression, self-confidence, and creative spirit. Improvisation stimulates interpretation of the music and reduces stage fright and inhibitions.

3. *Captivate the audience.* Create an entrance to capture their attention. Now start the combination, keeping the audience in mind. Use different levels, which means creating high, middle, and low movements. Make good use of your space by adding jumps and leaps. Bring yourself downstage. (Downstage is moving toward the audience, and upstage is moving away from the audience.) Try some floorwork, in which you get down on the floor. Be sure to stay in control and make your transitions smooth throughout.

4. *Apply style, flavor, and the spirit of the dance.* Use the music to help you add projection, energy, and attitude. Establish the mood or moods of the music. For example, when

creating a funk combination concentrate on the rhythms of the music. When creating a lyrical jazz combination, concentrate on the flow and mood of the music. Create with the lyrics; tell the story through movement. Vary the energy. Project an attitude. But overall, draw on VOP's essential elements to harmonize the movements.

VOP It: Spicing It Up With the Spirit of the Dance

Now it's time to apply the spirit of the dance. This process is like adding technicolor to your black and white combinations.

Following are sample combinations for each technical level to help you get started. After each combination we discuss the spirit of the dance and how to add style and flavor to each movement. Many different qualities can be expressed, depending on how the movements are connected together.

Sample Combination 1: Basic

In this combination for the beginner dancer, most of the movements have strong (whole) beats, with only a few syncopated ("&" count) beats. With the combination, we will review each movement, giving you tips to bring out the spirit of the dance.

When you create your own choreography, put any of the basic movements together. Feel free to use basic movements even for dancers who are more skilled. Don't try to create a masterpiece. Concentrate on making the movements flow together. Overall, just relax, let go, and feel the music. The stiffer you are, the harder it is to learn. But relaxing doesn't mean that it's okay to be sloppy—stay in control.

Here are Hatchett hints for applying the spirit of the dance to sample combination 1:

↻ **Step Touch:** Accent the arms on the reach up. Continue the energy through the fingertips. Accent the reach not the touch. Focus front. Don't look down.

Count	Movement	Level
12345678	Step Touch 4x's R, L, R, L	Basic
1234	Rib Reach 4x's R, L, R, L	Basic
5678	Reach Wrap R	Beginner
1234	Slice R to front L corner	Basic
5678	Step Pivot R to front and back corners	Basic
12	Walk front 2x's R, L	Basic
3&4	90s Jack	Beginner
5678	Shoulder bounces 4x's R, L, R, L	Basic
12345678	Raise the Roof 4x's R, L, R, L	Basic
1234	Cosmic Slop 2x's R, L	Basic
5678	Attitude Walk R around self	Basic
1&23&4	Run, Run, Run 2x's	Basic
5&67&8	Slap Wrap 2x's R, L	Basic
&12&34&56&78	Get Jiggy 4x's circling L	Basic
1	Strike R facing front	Basic

♻ **Rib Reach:** Accent the arms without hindering the rib cage from moving. Control the energy so you don't become stiff. Send the energy out through the fingertips.

♻ **Reach Wrap:** This movement has different body levels and energy qualities within it. Accent the reach to a high level, projecting front with attitude. Bend the knees to wrap R at a mid-level and project and focus R. Accent the reach side, and lift the heels to a high level while projecting front. Don't stop the energy at the wrists. Bend the knees to clap L at mid-level, and project and focus L.

♻ **Slice:** Add a bounce and let yourself go. Get funky. Create smooth energy. Relax and let the arms swing naturally. Project to the front corner not square front. Use the ball of the foot to touch back and rebound.

♻ **Step Pivot:** Accent the arms up with the knees bent, and stay low to the floor. Smooth out the energy as you pivot.

Frank Hatchett is an inspiration to any dancer serious about the jazz dance art form. His ability to encourage and energize his dancers and students to do their best is legendary, his expectations high. Thank you, Frank, for sharing with us your knowledge, beliefs, love of the art of dance, and your special brand of magic . . . VOP!

Sharon Wong, teacher and choreographer

♻ **Walk front:** Project front and walk with attitude.

♻ **90s Jack:** Be light on your feet, but don't bobble up and down. Give attitude.

♻ **Shoulder Bounces:** Relax and let it go. Have fun with it. Bend the knees and move lower to the floor (optional).

♻ **Raise the Roof:** Add a bounce. Feel the music. Smooth out the energy. Project front not up. Push the arms up.

♻ **Cosmic Slop:** Accent the arms side. Send energy into the floor without getting stuck. Make the transition smooth when you hop to bring the feet together.

♻ **Attitude Walk:** Get sassy and give loads of attitude. As you walk around, project front until you can't anymore. Then turn your head and project front again. Smooth out the energy and feel the walk.

♻ **Run, Run, Run:** This move is syncopated. Let it go and be light on the feet.

⟳ **Slap Wrap:** The slap is smooth, staying low to the floor. Project over the R knee. Accent the wrap and give attitude. Project front.

⟳ **Get Jiggy:** This move is a total groove thing. It comes from within. Keep it syncopated.

⟳ **Strike:** Accent the arms and a head snap side, giving the audience loads of attitude.

Sample Combination 2: Beginner

This combination for beginners and advanced beginners has more syncopated movements than the basic combination in sample 1. Notice that the whole combination is not syncopated. This gives the combination more flavor and dimension and is the start to great choreography. This prevents a dance from becoming monotonous. Again, be sure to use your whole space. Overall, just relax, let go, and feel the music. Once you feel comfortable, you're ready to add the spirit of the dance.

Here are Hatchett hints for applying the spirit of the dance to sample combination 2:

⟳ **Attitude Walk:** Get sassy and give the audience loads of attitude. Project front. Smooth the energy and feel confident.

⟳ **Three-Step Throw:** This movement contains different body levels and energy qualities. Stretch strong arms overhead to a high level while projecting front with attitude. Don't burst the energy; keep it smooth. Send energy out through the fingertips. Bend the knees to a low level while throwing the arms. Stay in control. Project out and snap the head in the direction of the arms.

⟳ **Cookies n' Milk:** Feel the groove coming from within. Add a bounce, and bend the knees. Project up to the front R corner.

⟳ **Pas de Bourrée:** Stay light on the feet with smooth energy.

⟳ **Snake:** Relax and let it go. The head starts the snake. It's a ripple move with smooth energy.

⟳ **Jump Touch:** Add a bounce. Get funky. Relax and let the torso move.

⟳ **Window Wash:** Relax, let it go, and move the hips. Project front with personality.

Count	Movement	Level
1234	Attitude Walk front 4x's R, L, R, L	Basic
5&67&8	Three-Step Throw 2x's R, L	Beginner
1&2&3&4&	Cookies n' Milk R 2x's	Beginner
5&67&8	Pas De Bourrée 2x's R, L	Basic
&12&34&56&78	Snake 4x's R, L, R, L	Beginner
&1&2&3&4&5&6&7&8	Jump Touch 2x's R-L-R-R, L-R-L-L	Basic
123&4567&8	Window Wash 2x's R, L	Beginner
1&2&3&4	Syncopated Jacks	Adv. Beginner
&5&6&7&8	Whack, Whack 2x's	Adv. Beginner
123	Step R, Cross L, Step R	All
&4&5&6	Hitch Kick R 2x's	Adv. Beginner
78	Step R, Throw L	Var. of Basic
1&2&3&4&	Hip Pulses 4x's	Beginner
5&67&8	Heel Dig 2x's R, L	Adv. Beginner
1	Step to second with V-Position Arms	Basic

Be light on the feet, and make a smooth transition into the pas de bourrée.

↺ **Syncopated Jacks:** This move is syncopated. Be light on the feet, but don't bobble up and down. This movement stays at one level. Don't get stuck on the wrap.

↺ **Whack, Whack:** Relax and keep the hands in fists. The energy is smooth. Add a bounce with the knees bent. Be prepared to transition into the next movement (step, cross, step).

↺ **Step, Cross, Step:** This is a traveling movement into the Hitch Kick.

↺ **Hitch Kick:** Project to the front R corner. Kick with strong energy, but still control the body.

↺ **Step, Throw:** Project out and snap the head L in the direction of the arm throw. Send energy out through the fingertips.

↺ **Hip Pulses:** Project front. Hip pulse to the front R corner. Relax and let the torso and shoulders move. The energy is smooth.

↺ **Heel Dig:** Release the torso and lean back to rebound front. Smooth the energy. Control it.

↺ **Step to second with V-Position Arms:** Hit the V with a burst of energy and strong arms; project front.

Sample Combination 3: Intermediate/Advanced

This combination has a lot more syncopated movements than in sample combination 2. When creating choreography at this level, fuse together moves for different ability levels, styles, and moods to create interesting combinations. Also incorporate floor work, and experiment with patterns. Once you have

Count	Movements	Level
123&4&5&6&78	Footwork	Int/Advanced
12&3&456&7&8	Syncopated Grapevine 2x's R, L	Int/Advanced
123&da4567&da8	Kibee Kibee 2x's R, L	Int/Advanced
123&4567&8	Reach Pull Pas de Bourrée Turn 2x's R, L	Int/Advanced
1&2&3&4&5&6&7&8	Homework Coordination Step	Int/Advanced
&1&2&3&4&5&6&7&8	Hatchett Walk 2x's R, L	Adv. Beginner
12&34	Turning Stag Leap	Int/Advanced
567&8	Battement Passé R to front corner, end facing back corner, hold, ball change	Int/Advanced
12	Walk forward 2x's R, L to back L corner	Basic
3&4	Grand Jeté R to back L corner	Int/Advanced
5678	Attitude Turn R end front	Int/Advanced
1&23&45&67&8	Sugar 4x's R, L, R, L traveling to front R corner	Basic
12345678	90s Chug 4x's R, L, R, L to front	Beginner
&12	Ball change R, hold	All
34	Outside Parallel Turn R	Int/Advanced
56	Whack, Whack jumping from second to first	Adv. Beginner
78	Whip R, Strike L	Basic
123&4	Turning Axle Jump R	Int/Advanced
5&6	Pas de Bourrée Turn L	Var. of Basic
7&8	Second Jump	Int/Advanced

created the combination, apply the spirit of the dance. Always concentrate on your technique, but don't stifle the feeling and the marriage between the music and the movement. Dance it!

↻ **Attitude Turn:** Change focus to spot the front. Sustain the turn by lifting up, with energy continuing through the fingertips. Continue to lift up as you land from the turn.

↻ **Sugar:** It's a groove from within. Project and travel to the front corner. Add a bounce and let it go while staying in control. Relax the shoulders to allow the rib cage more mobility.

↻ **90s Chug:** Project front and stay light on the feet. Let it go and feel the groove. Bend the knees and lean the torso forward.

↻ **Hold, Ball Change:** This move prepares you for the Outside Turn. Don't wind up.

Meeting Frank Hatchett literally changed the course of my life. Through dance training at his school, Frank instilled a confidence that I still benefit from to this day. I'll always be grateful for the opportunities and doors he helped open for me. I'll never forget the lessons learned, the tears shed, or the pains shared while a student at his school.

Bruce Goolsby

↻ **Outside Parallel Turn:** Everything happens in the turn at once—the attachment of the foot, the movement of the arms, and the spotting. Watch your timing. Only complete enough turns to be on the proper beat for the next movement (Whack, Whack).

↻ **Whack, Whack:** Take a small jump into second. Let it go, keeping the hands in fists.

↻ **Whip, Strike:** Bend the knees and get down on the whip. Accent the strike with a head snap and attitude.

↻ **Turning Axle Jump:** Use a middle level for the chaîné. Lift the energy through the chest and arms on the turn. Project side when you land without dropping your energy.

↻ **Pas de Bourrée Turn:** Keep the momentum going out of the last jump and into the turn.

↻ **Second Jump:** Make a smooth transition from the turn into the Second Jump. Lift the energy through the chest and out through the fingertips. Continue to lift up as you land out of the jump.

Here are Hatchett hints for applying the spirit of the dance to sample combination 3:

↻ **Footwork:** The Footwork is syncopated with smooth energy. Different feelings can be applied within the movement. Flick and hold with attitude. Stay light on the feet for the rest of the movement. Don't get stuck in the ball change. Rebound the energy to walk front.

↻ **Syncopated Grapevine:** It's quick, light, and syncopated with controlled energy.

↻ **Kibee, Kibee:** This move is syncopated. Feel the rhythm from within, so it naturally shows on your face. If you're really into it, the feeling can't help but show.

↻ **Reach Pull Pas de Bourrée turn:** It's syncopated. Let the energy go for the reach, then control your energy for the turn to make a smooth transition.

↻ **Hatchett Walk:** The walk is a groove with smooth energy. You should feel as though you're gliding across the floor.

↻ **Homework Coordination Step:** This step is quick but smooth. Control your energy by placing your arms.

↻ **Turning Stag Leap:** Use a middle level height for the chaîné and then burst with energy into the Stag Leap. Project front.

↻ **Battement Passé:** Make the kick strong without losing control. Project out to the corner. Smooth out the energy while transitioning to the turn and projecting to the back corner. Lift up to control your balance.

↻ **Walks:** Don't drop the energy after the Battement Passé. These walks are your preparation for the next movement (Grand Jeté).

↻ **Grand Jeté:** Burst with energy as you jump off the floor, lifting through the chest and arms to suspend the body in the air. Keep the back leg up by sending energy out the foot. Don't drop the energy as you land from the leap; keep it going for the next movement (Attitude Turn).

Final Thoughts

The following concepts can help enhance the dance experience for dancers at all ability levels.

1. *Add changes to a combination to make the mind think more quickly.* Adding changes really helps the creative process. Practice the movements by changing the sequence of the combination. If you keep reviewing the same movements in the same sequence and then add on, you won't improve your ability to pick up as quickly. Mixing up a combination makes the dance exciting and fun because it's familiar but at the same time challenging. Over time, you will learn the movement, while keeping your mind alert to any changes. This will help you begin to pick up combinations more quickly. This ability will be a tremendous asset should you ever go to an audition and makes taking class a lot more fun.

2. *Break down the movement, but don't overdo it.* You need to break down the movements so you can understand the counts, timing, and quality. Your objective is to make the steps flow musically. Breaking down the movement allows you to incorporate the spirit of the dance. If you break the movement down too much, however, you risk making it looking rigid, choppy, and disjointed.

3. *Thinking, feeling, and dancing are one.* Dancers often think too much, which can slow down their timing and movement. Don't let the thinking override the feeling. Thinking, feeling, and dancing all work together. Not allowing thinking to overwhelm your dancing helps you to pull the feeling from within, naturally, instinctively. It will also make your dancing more fluid. The most important thing to remember is to relax and let go of your inhibitions. Loosen up and feel the music. Train yourself to think fast and to keep your mind clear and focused. This will help you to pick up movements more quickly and keep your energy level high.

4. *Challenge yourself, but know your limitations.* Challenging yourself is essential to developing into a great dancer. Equally important is knowing when you have reached your limits (for example, messing up at the same spot consecutively). Try not to dwell on or compound your frustrations; keep the combinations moving and energetic. As you become more confident, you will be able to do more challenging movements.

5. *Do not always depend on the mirror.* The mirror is an excellent tool for learning, but it can become a crutch. You can become dependent on visualizing, not thinking and feeling. You will have difficulty assuming the correct focus (what direction you're looking), which helps in executing the movements properly. Also, learn to become comfortable facing all directions of the room. This will give you confidence when performing on stage. Try switching a combination to face the back so you can practice dancing without a mirror.

6. *Don't be afraid to take a chance.* Challenge yourself at the end of the combination by adding a more difficult movement. Take the chance even though you may not perfect it at first. At least you're attempting it. Push yourself to reach your fullest potential.

7. *Cool down after dancing.* Don't just stop, have a drink, and sit down. Take five minutes to return your muscles to a pre-dance state.

> Frank is more than just a dance teacher. His energy and drive have motivated many young, talented people and his dedication has inspired me to make giving back to the community a priority in my life.
> *Monife Marshall, Affiliate Manager, Black Entertainment Television, Inc.*

Do a few rhythmic exercises followed by some stretching. Taking the time to cool down will leave you feeling great and prevent the risk of injury.

So now you have it . . . our "inside story" for learning how to make the Hatchett style come alive. The artistic impression of jazz dance is enhanced through the freedom, spirit, and beauty of the dancer. We hope that you have enjoyed using this book as a learning or teaching tool (or both). Ultimately we hope you had an opportunity to enjoy the unique experience of VOP.

Remember, reach for the moon and you'll always be among the stars.

Dance Finder

The Dance Finder will help you locate VOP movements based on certain criteria. Movements are listed in alphabetical order and are checked according to the following categories: level, type of movement, and style.

Use the Dance Finder when you choreograph phrases and combinations to help you find the perfect moves to fit your mood, music, and personal style. Be sure to fuse each movement with the spirit of the dance and VOP it.

Movement	Level	Street/hip hop	Syncopated	Travel	Body/hand/arm positions	Walks	Jumps/leaps	Turns
Afro chug (133)	Int/adv		X	X				
Afro crosswalks (67)	Basic			X		X		
Afro side step (99)	Beg							
Attitude turn (134)	Int/adv							X
Attitude walk (68)	Basic			X		X		
Battement passé turn (135)	Int/adv							X
Bow and arrow (100)	Beg			X				
Brazilian samba (136)	Int/adv							
Butterfly (69)	Basic	X						
Cabbage patch (70)	Basic	X						
Choo choo (101)	Beg							
Contemporary wrap (71)	Basic				X			
Cookies n' milk (102)	Beg							
Cool walk (137)	Int/adv			X		X		
Cosmic slop (72)	Basic	X						
Coupé turn (138)	Int/adv							X
Cut (73)	Basic				X			
Dig swivel (74)	Basic							X
Flamenco attitude (119)	Adv beg		X					
Flick (75)	Basic					X		
Footwork (139)	Int/adv		X					
Giddy up (120)	Adv beg							
Get jiggy (76)	Basic	X						
Grand jeté (142)	Int/adv			X			X	
Hatchett walk (121)	Adv beg			X		X		X
Heel dig (122)	Adv beg							
Heel twist (123)	Adv beg							
Hip pulses (103)	Beg							
Hitch kick (124)	Adv beg						X	
Homework coordination step (140)	Int/adv							
Inside-outside parallel turns (143)	Int/adv							X
Jazz hand (77)	Basic				X			
Jazz stance (78)	Basic				X			
Jazz wrist press (79)	Basic				X			
Jump touch (80)	Basic							
Kibee kibee (144)	Int/adv		X					
Layout (145)	Int/adv							
90s camel walk (146)	Int/adv			X		X		
90s chug (104)	Beg							
90s jack (105)	Beg							

166

Movement	Level	Street/ hip hop	Syncopated	Travel	Body/hand/ arm positions	Walks	Jumps/ leaps	Turns
Pas de bourrée (81)	Basic							
Penguin (106)	Beg							
Pump (147)	Int/adv							
Raise the roof (82)	Basic	X						
Reach pull cha, cha, cha (83)	Basic		X					
Reach pull pas de bourrée turn (148)	Int/adv		X					X
Reach pull pas de bourrée (125)	Adv beg		X					
Reach wrap (107)	Beg							
Rib reach (84)	Basic							
Rhythmic shoulder push (149)	Int/adv							
Running man (108)	Beg	X						
Run, run, run (85)	Basic	X						
Salsa (150)	Int/adv							
Salsa footwork (151)	Int/adv							
Second jump (152)	Int/adv			X			X	
Shimmy pivot chug (126)	Adv beg							
Shoulder bounces (86)	Basic							
Sky to earth (109)	Beg							
Slap wrap (87)	Basic							
Slice (88)	Basic							
Snake (110)	Beg	X						
Step pivot (89)	Basic							
Step touch (90)	Basic							
Strike (91)	Basic				X			
Sugar (92)	Basic							
Syncopated jacks (127)	Adv beg		X					
Syncopated grapevine (153)	Int/adv		X	X				
Three-step throw (111)	Beg			X				
Throw, throw (93)	Basic							
Triple shoulders (112)	Beg							
Turning axle jump (154)	Int/adv						X	X
Turning stag leap (155)	Int/adv						X	X
Under pump (128)	Adv beg	X						
VOP windmill (113)	Beg							
V-position arms (94)	Basic				X			
Whack, whack (129)	Adv beg	X						
Whip (95)	Basic							
Window wash (114)	Beg		X					

Dance Terms

arabesque: Body position in which the arms and legs are extended. Lift one leg straight back with the weight on the supporting leg. Various arm positions can be used.

arm positions: The following positions are from the French and Russian ballet schools:

1st position—Round the arms in front of chest.

2nd position—Reach the arms side.

5th position—Round the arms overhead.

barre: Long rounded piece of wood that attaches to the wall or is freestanding. The dancer performs exercises at the barre, which can be used as an aide for learning more complex feet patterns.

battement: Lift one leg up forcefully in air, then control the leg down while the torso remains straight.

chaîné: Turning movement, in which the dancer executes a half turn on each foot. Spotting (focusing on an object, then snapping the head around and focusing on the object again) is required.

changement: Jump with straight legs turned out and pressed together and changing feet in the air. It's easiest to start in fifth position.

chassé: Step one foot side, step the other foot next to it, then step the first foot side again. One foot leads and the other chases it. This can be executed in any direction.

coupé: Bend the working leg with a pointed foot, and lift the leg until the foot meets the front of the supporting ankle.

coupé turn: Turn with the working held in the coupé position.

demi-plié parallel: Bend the knees halfway, keeping the heels on the floor. Legs and feet face front in parallel position.

demi-plié turned out: Bend the knees halfway, keeping the heels on the floor. Legs and feet turn out from the hips.

demi-pointe: Rise up on ball of the foot.

développé: Bend the working leg with a pointed foot and lift the leg until the foot meets the side of the supporting leg. Then extend the working leg straight front. This can be done in any direction.

grand jeté: Execute a front-split jump in the air. Push off back foot and land on front foot then bring the other foot down.

grand plié: Bend the knees fully with the heels lifted. Legs and feet turn out from the hips.

pas de bourrée turn: Make a full turn in one direction as you execute three quick steps. Keep the weight over the balls of the feet. Start with your feet together. Cross the R foot behind the L and start turning R, step the L foot front facing back, step the R foot front facing front.

passé parallel: Bend the working leg with a pointed foot, and lift the leg until the arch of the foot meets the side of the knee on the supporting leg. Legs and feet face front.

passé turned out: Bend the working leg with a pointed foot, and lift the leg until the toe meets the side of the supporting leg. Legs and feet turn out from the hips.

relevé: Raise the heel and arch while the ball of the foot remains in contact with the floor.

Bibliography

Ballet Is Fun. 1995–96. An Interactive CD-ROM Video Dictionary. Business Works, Inc.

Encyclopaedia Britannica Guide to Black History. [Online], s.v. "Dunham, Katherine." Available: http://blackhistory.eb.com:80/micro/180/95.html [May 5, 1999].

Grant, Gail. 1967. *Technical Manual and Dictionary of Classical Ballet.* New York: Dover Publications.

Greenhill, Janet. 1993. "Treat People Nicely: Give Them a Great Class." *Dance Teacher Now* 15(5): 32–42.

Larkin, Marilynn. 1986. "Hatchett Is Hot." *Dance Teacher Now* 8(6): 10–15.

Rogosin, Elinor. 1997. "Frank Hatchett: In Conversation." *The Dancer* January.

Quilter, Deborah. 1997. "Jazz It Up: Seven Secrets From Frank Hatchett, the King of 'VOP.'" *Dance Spirit* 1(2): 78.

About the Authors

Frank Hatchett

Nancy Myers Gitlin

Loved and admired throughout the world for his unique style of jazz dance and inspirational teaching, **Frank Hatchett** is quite simply one of the legendary jazz dance masters. Hatchett is currently the dean of dance at the prestigious Broadway Dance Center in New York City where more than 250,000 dancers come to learn each year. He's had an impressive roster of students, including Madonna, Brooke Shields, Naomi Campbell, Olivia Newton-John, Justine Bateman, Vanessa Williams, Julie Brown, Suzette Charles, Savion Glover, and dozens of Broadway and daytime television actors and actresses.

Dubbed "The Doctor of Jazz" by ABC's *Good Morning America,* Frank Hatchett has a very high-profile career. He's been featured on the Emmy Award-winning CNBC episode of *Real Stories* and spotlighted on MTV's show *The Real World.* He has also received the prestigious L'Hult D'Or Award from Paris. Hatchett teaches classes throughout the country at national dance conventions but calls New York City home.

Nancy Myers Gitlin has been a student of Frank Hatchett's for over 30 years. She graduated from the Boston Conservatory of Music with a BFA in dance and has taught at Broadway Dance Center, the Boston Conservatory of Music, Johnson County Community College, and numerous dance studios.

Gitlin has developed college dance curriculums and is currently on the dance faculty at Lake Michigan College. She is also dance/fitness coordinator at the YMCA Family Center in St. Joseph, Michigan, where she resides with her husband and two children.

Use imagery and improvisation to enrich your repertoire

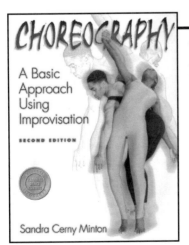